# Venice

**by Teresa Fisher**

Teresa Fisher is a freelance travel writer who has contributed to a number of newspaper and magazines at home and abroad, as well as writing a variety of AA publications, including CityPack Amsterdam, Essential Barcelona, Spiral Guide to Paris and Spiral Guide Florence.

Above: *View from the Grand Canal at night*

**AA Publishing**

**Written by Teresa Fisher; 'Peace & Quiet' by Paul Sterry**
Contributions to this edition by
Hilary Weston and Jackie Staddon

*Gondoliers are identified by their distinctive boater hats*

First published 1991
Revised second edition 1995
Revised third edition 2000
Reprinted May, Sept 2001
Reprinted June 2002; April 2003
**This edition 2006. Information verified and updated.**
Reprinted Apr and Aug 2006
Reprinted Feb and May 2007



Published by AA Publishing, a trading name of Automobile Association Developments Limited, whose registered office is Fanum House, Basing View, Basingstoke, Hampshire RG21 4EA. Registered number 1878835.



A CIP catalogue record for this book is available from the British Library.



The contents of this publication are believed correct at the time of printing. Nevertheless, AA Publishing accepts no responsibility for any errors, omissions or changes in the details given, nor for the consequences of readers' reliance on this information. This does not affect your statutory rights. Assessments of the attractions and hotels and restaurants are based upon the author's own experience and contain subjective opinions that may not reflect the publisher's opinion or a reader's experience.

We have tried to ensure accuracy, but things do change, so please let us know if you have any comments or corrections.

Find out more about AA Publishing and the wide range of travel publications and services the AA provides by visiting our website at www.theAA.com/travel

A03454

Colour separation: Keenes, Andover
Printed and bound in Italy by Printer Trento S.r.l.

# Contents

# About this Book

**KEY TO SYMBOLS**

- map reference to the maps found in the What to See section
- address or location
- telephone number
- opening times
- restaurant or café on premises or nearby
- nearest underground train station
- nearest bus/tram route
- nearest overground train station
- nearest riverboat or ferry stops
- travel by air
- tourist information
- facilities for visitors with disabilities
- admission charge
- other places of interest nearby
- other practical information
- indicates the page where you will find a fuller description

This book is divided into five sections to cover the most important aspects of your visit to Venice.

**Viewing Venice** pages 5–14
An introduction to Venice by the author.
Venice's Features
Essence of Venice
The Shaping of Venice
Peace and Quiet
Venice's Famous

**Top Ten** pages 15–26
The author's choice of the Top Ten places to see in Venice, listed in alphabetical order, each with practical information.

**What to See** pages 27–90
Two sections: Venice and Excursions from Venice, each with its own brief introduction and an alphabetical listing of the main attractions.
Practical information
Snippets of 'Did you know…' information
3 suggested walks
2 suggested boat trips
2 features

**Where To…** pages 91–116
Detailed listings of the best places to eat, stay, shop, take the children and be entertained.

**Practical Matters** pages 117–124
A highly visual section containing essential travel information.

**Maps**
All map references are to the individual maps found in the What to See section of this guide.
For example, Basilica di San Marco has the reference 29D2—indicating the page on which the map is located and the grid square in which the castle is to be found. A list of the maps that have been used in this travel guide can be found in the index.

**Prices**
Where appropriate, an indication of the cost of an establishment is given by **€** signs:
**€€€** denotes higher prices, **€€** denotes average prices, while **€** denotes lower charges.

**Star Ratings**
Most of the places described in this book have been given a separate rating:

Do not miss
Highly recommended
Worth seeing

# Viewing Venice



*Gondolas awaiting passengers on the Grand Canal*

# Teresa Fisher's Venice

### Getting Your Bearings

Venice is divided into six *sestieri*: San Marco, San Polo, Santa Croce, Dorsoduro, Cannaregio and Castello. Two natural waterways define the city—the Grand Canal, which coils snake-like, dividing the city into two, and the Giudecca shipping channel to the south.

### Gondolas

Gondolas were first recorded in 1904. In the 18th century there were 14,000 in use. Today there are around 400, all made to the same design: 10.87m (35ft 6in) in length, with a maximum width of 1.42m (4ft 6in). The hull is asymmetrical—24cm (approx 9in) wider on the left than on the right—to assist with steerage. Each gondola is made out of 280 parts, made from eight different woods—fir, cherry, walnut, larch, mahogany, oak, lime and elm—and, according to 16th-century law, are all painted with seven layers of black lacquer.

*The reflective beauty of Venice*

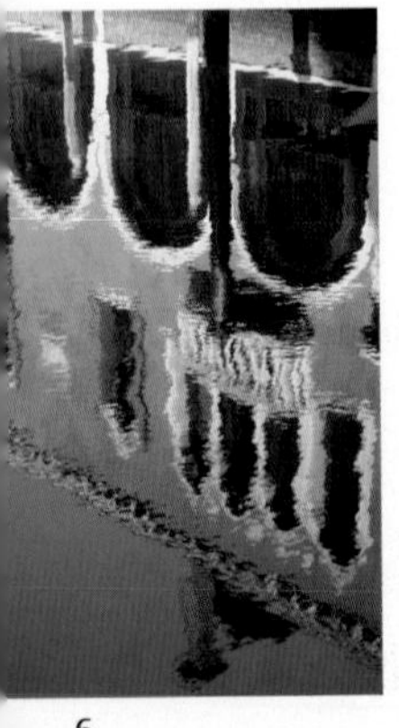

For centuries Venetians and visitors alike have been spell-bound by Venice, It is the most breathtakingly beautiful and extraordinary city, equal parts stone and water; a floating city laid out on some 40 tiny islands with 'the sea for its floor, the sky for its roof, and the flow of water for walls' (Boncompagno da Signa, 1240).

Even though it has been painted, photographed, written about and filmed more than any other city in the world, nothing can prepare you for the first powerful impact of Venice. It may be a gondola down the Grand Canal when the city is enveloped in the mists of winter or when the setting of the summer sun bathes the city in the magical pinks, blues and golds so beloved by artists such as Titian, Veronese and Canaletto, but it is guaranteed that your first impressions will be memorable. And there is so much more behind the famous icons. Scratch beneath the surface to discover a myriad of sights to tempt the senses.

Few cities can offer such artistic richness as Venice. For many centuries, as the gateway to the Orient and under the medieval leadership of the doges (dukes), the city ruled as a world capital and a mighty sea power, and its immense wealth was celebrated in art and architecture. Today, with the glories of this heritage evident at every turn, you could easily mistake Venice for a painting come alive, a stage set full of real people, an open-air museum.

Venice is no museum but rather a living and fragile city; it is a miracle of survival despite its decaying foundations, the encroaching water and rising silt. Although, contrary to popular belief, it is officially 'no longer sinking', its ominously tilting bell towers stand as testimony to the city's ephemerality, as concerns mount about increasing levels of pollution from nearby industrial towns, which are irreperably corroding the city's ancient stonework. This is to say nothing of the rapidly dwindling population as modern houses, jobs, plans for a metro and other attempts to preserve Venice for the Venetians clash with those aimed at preserving the city for posterity.

When you leave Venice, your memories will not only be of its beauty and art treasures but also of city life—pasta alfresco in a peaceful sun-splashed piazza, the gentle swaying of gondolas tied to gaily striped mooring poles, the sights and scents of local markets, buildings reflected in the still water of the canals, shop windows brimming with Carnival masks and dazzling glass displays or even Piazza San Marco (St. Mark's Square) flooded on a high tide. This is the magic of Venice, which entices devoted visitors back year after year to *La Serenissima*—the 'most serene', and captivating, city in the world.

# Venice's Features

## The City

- Height above sea level: 80cm (31in)
- Height of 1966 floods: 2m (6ft)
- Highest point: Campanile at 99m (325ft)
- Size of city (from east to west): 5km (3 miles)
- Size of city (from north to south): 2km (1 mile)
- Size eqivalent to: Central Park, New York
- Number of districts (*sestieri*): 6
- Number of canals: 170
- Number of bridges (estimated): 400
- Number of alleys (estimated): 3,000
- Number of churches (estimated): 200
- Rate of sinking (annual): 0cm (no longer sinking)
- Buildings on Grand Canal with damaged foundations: 60 per cent
- Visitors per year (estimated): between 13 and 14 million

*Wisteria on a building in the Cannaregio district*

## Population

- Population in heyday of Venetian Republic (estimated): 200,000
- Population in 1950 (estimated): 140,000
- Population in 1998 (estimated): 68,000
- People leaving Venice annually due to high prices, lack of jobs and housing (estimated): 1,500

## Economic Factors

- Cost of living: 1 per cent higher than Milan, 3 per cent higher than Rome
- Percentage of workforce involved in tourism: over 50 per cent
- Number of gift shops (estimated): 450
- Number of plumbers (estimated): 13

## The Lagoon

- Length: 56km (30 miles)
- Width: 8–14km (5–9 miles)
- Surface area: 550sq km (212sq miles)

*View towards the Campanile in Piazza San Marco*

# Essence of Venice

Venice is a city that charms and captivates, the historic flagship of a mighty fleet of islands in the lagoon, the most photogenic city in the world. To discover its true character you should first see the main sights—the Grand Canal, St. Mark's Square, the Doges' Palace. But then take time to explore the picture-postcard backwaters with their hidden squares and tiny churches. There's a secret side to Venice too, only accessible by water. Once afloat, you enter a different world, seeing the city as it was designed to be seen—through snatched glimpses into ancient houses, secluded gardens and boatyards with gondolas waiting for repair. This is where the real essence of Venice lies.

*Gondolas ply the choppy water in front on Santa Maria della Salute*

## THE 10 ESSENTIALS

*If you only have a short time to visit Venice or would like to get a really complete picture of the city, here are the essentials:*

• **Take a boat** (and plenty of film!) along the Grand Canal by day to marvel at its majestic water-lapped palaces and gaily painted mooring poles or by night to catch glimpses of the grand illuminated interiors.

• **Visit the Rialto markets** (► 43) at the crack of dawn before the crowds arrive.

• **A mid-morning coffee** in Europe's finest square, atmospheric Piazza San Marco (► 21), will both delight and bankrupt you.

• **Stroll along the southern shore** of the Dorsoduro, with its boathouses, bars and cafés. Go at dusk, when Venetians take their *passeggiata* (evening stroll).

• **Indulge yourself** in the romance of a gondola ride at sunset and capture the true magic of Venice.

• **Take the lift** up to the top of the Campanile (► 35) or San Giorgio Maggiore (► 22) for breathtaking views.

• **Watch the world go by** from the terrace of a Venetian classic, Harry's Bar, whilst sipping on a Bellini cocktail (► 114).

• **Get lost in the labyrinthine alleys** and backwaters of the city, or visit the outlying islands (► 76–83) for a taste of Venetian life off the main tourist drag.

• **See Venice by night.** The canals have a magical beauty and many of the main monuments are floodlit.

• **End your day Venetian-style** with an ice cream or a *digestif* (liqueur) in one of the city's countless café-ringed squares. One of the best ice-cream shops is Paolin (► 98).

Above: *Relaxing at Café Florian in Piazza San Marco*
Below: *Shopping in the Rialto Market*

# The Shaping of Venice

*Venetian galleys are loaded up by crusaders embarking on the Fourth Crusade*

**8th century BC**
The Veneti and Euganei tribes are the first to settle in the lagoon area.

**3rd century BC**
Veneto conquered by the Romans.

**AD402**
Alaric the Goth sacks Altinium; its inhabitants flee to the lagoon, guided by a vision of the Virgin Mary.

**421**
According to legend, Venice is founded on 25 March.

**453**
Attila the Hun sacks Aquileia, prompting another exodus of refugees to the lagoon.

**466**
Lagoon's settlements elect 'maritime tribunes' to govern.

**697**
Maritime tribunes appoint the first Doge (leader) of Venice—Paoluccio Anafesto.

**814**
First Venetian coins minted. Work begins on the Doges' Palace.

**828**
Venetian merchants steal the relics of St. Mark from Alexandria.

**829**
Work commences on the Basilica di San Marco.

**1000**
'The Marriage to the Sea' ceremony (➤ 116) is inaugurated to celebrate Doge Pietro Orseolo II's defeat of Dalmatian pirates in the Adriatic.

**1094**
Basilica di San Marco is consecrated.

**1095**
Venice provides ships for the First Crusade.

**1204**
Venice sacks Constantinople in the Fourth Crusade and acquires much of the former Byzantine Empire.

**1271**
Marco Polo leaves Venice for the Far East.

**1348**
The Black Death kills half the population.

**1380**
The Battle of Chioggia: Venice defeats the Genoese, thereby proving its unrivalled maritime supremacy in both the Adriatic and Mediterranean seas.

**1406**
Venice defeats Padua and Verona to lay the foundations of a mainland empire.

**1450**
Venice's power reaches its height.

**1453**
Constantinople falls to the Turks, ending Venice's trading privileges.

**1514**
Fire destroys the original timber Rialto bridge.

**1571**
Venice loses Cyprus to the Turks but Battle of Lepanto is decisive victory for the western fleet, including Venice.

**1669**
Venice loses Crete to the Turks.

**1678**
Vivaldi is born in Venice. He teraches violin at the La Pietà orphanage.

**1718**
Surrender of Morea to the Turks marks the end of the Venetian maritime empire.

**1752**
Completion of sea walls protecting the lagoon entrances.

**1797**
Napoleon invades Italy; the last doge abdicates and the Venetian Republic comes to an end.

**1814**
Following Napoleon's defeat Venice and the Veneto are ceded to Austria.

**1846**
Rail causeway links Venice to the mainland for the first time.

**1848**
First Italian War of Independence. Venice revolts against Austrian rule.

**1866**
Venice joins a united Italy.

**1881**
Venice becomes the second largest port in Italy after Genoa.

*The Rialto Bridge*

**1895**
First Biennale art exhibition.

**1902**
The Campanile in Piazza San Marco collapses (rebuilt by 1912).

**1932**
First Venice Film Festival.

**1960**
The new Venice airport opens.

**1966**
Floods cause devastation. UNESCO launches its 'Save Venice' appeal.

**1973**
Laws passed to reduce pollution, subsidence and flooding.

**1978**
Patriarch Luciani of Venice elected Pope John Paul I, but dies 33 days later.

**1983**
Venice officially stops sinking (after extraction of underground water is prohibited).

**1988**
Work begins on the lagoon's flood barrier.

**1995**
Centenary of Biennale Exhibition.

**2003**
The controversial MOSE project is set up; mobile flood barriers to prevent further damage to the vunerable buildings.

# Peace & Quiet

## Countryside and Wildlife around Venice by Paul Sterry

For an island city so completely dominated by buildings, Venice might seem an unpromising destination for the holiday naturalist. Venice and the Veneto coast have considerable wildlife interest, and the city makes a good base from which to explore the watery habitat surrounding it. Venice lies in the Laguna Veneta, a marine lagoon near the mouth of the River Po, which is almost completely cut off from the sea by sand bars. The lagoon is studded with islands and salt marsh, the whole area being a haven for wildlife, in particular birds. Ducks, waders, egrets and herons are all numerous at certain times of the year. Although much of the Po delta and Laguna Veneta are inaccessible, many species can be seen during boat trips or from the adjacent mainland. By way of a complete contrast, those who want a few days' break from Venice can make a comparatively short journey north through sunny hillsides to the Italian Alps.

*Peahen on the islet of San Francesco del Deserto*

## Venice and the Venetian Lagoon

Visitors to Venice might be forgiven for supposing that, after people, pigeons and cats are not just the commonest residents of the city but its only living inhabitants. However true this might seem at first glance, a more thorough tour of even the city itself will turn up a surprising number of birds, and a boat tour to one of the other islands is sure to enthral.

Parks and gardens, however small, in the quieter backstreets of Venice are likely to host serins. These delightful little relatives of the canary sing a beautiful, twittering song throughout spring and early summer, usually from the topmost branches of a tree. Search the lower branches and dense foliage of bushes and you may find a variety of warblers; melodious warblers, blackcaps, lesser whitethroats and even

Sardinian warblers can all be seen. Although the spring migration period is the best time of year for seeing these birds, some of them linger on into the summer months.

Black redstarts are also found in parks and gardens but are equally at home on the roofs of houses. Some species can become quite confiding and seem not to be bothered at all by people. Gulls frequent the shores of the lagoon and sometimes congregate where boats and larger ships are moored. The yellow-legged race of herring gull is most often seen in the winter months, but black-headed gulls are frequent year round. Scrutinise each one carefully because the somewhat similar Mediterranean gull is also often numerous. In its summer plumage, this is one of the most elegant of gulls and sports a black hood, red eye-ring and pure white wings. It has a distinctive 'cow-cow' call.

Boat trips between the islands in the Laguna Veneta pass the occasional undisturbed shoreline and areas of reed bed. Waders, grey herons and little egrets, the latter species easily recognised by its white plumage, black legs and bright yellow feet, prefer the open shores. Marsh harriers, reed warblers, buntings and purple herons, on the other hand, prefer the sanctuary provided by the reeds. Unfortunately, boat trips generally offer only fleeting glimpses of these habitats and to study them in more detail it is probably best to return to mainland Italy and explore the Po delta from there.

*Looking across the lagoon*

# Venice's Famous

## Marco Polo

Marco Polo was born in Venice in 1254. At the age of 18 he set out with his merchant father on a four-year overland voyage to the court of Mongol prince Kublai Khan. Here he worked as a diplomat for 17 years, travelling through China and the Far East, returning home in 1295. Three years later he was captured by the Genoese at the Battle of Curzola. In prison, with the help of his cell mate, he put his adventures down on paper, and the *Description of the World* was for long Europe's most accurate account of the Far East. Once freed, he returned to Venice and died in 1324.

## Antonio Vivaldi

Vivaldi was born in Venice in 1678. Although ordained as a priest, he devoted his life to music, working as a violin teacher and choirmaster at the orphanage attached to the church of La Pietà (▶ 47). He wrote many of his finest pieces for La Pietà, including 454 concertos and the well-known *Four Seasons*, and the church became famous for its performances. However, music tastes changed and in 1740 Vivaldi left Venice to seek work in Vienna. He died a year later and was buried in a pauper's grave.

**An Honorary Venetian**
In 1949 Peggy Guggenheim, the famous American copper heiress and modern art collector, purchased the most eccentric palazzo on the Grand Canal to house her outstanding art collection and her retinue of poodles. An honorary citizen of the city, she stayed in Venice until her death in 1979 and is buried (together with her dogs) in the palazzo gardens.

## Giacomo Girolamo Casanova de Seingalt

Dubbed Italy's greatest lover, Casanova was born in Venice in 1725. Though destined for the priesthood, his dissolute behaviour led to his expulsion from the seminary. Exiled from Venice for five years, he soon discovered his real vocation in the bedrooms of Europe and was in due course forced to flee Paris, Vienna, Dresden and Prague as a result of various scandals. Returning to Venice in 1755, he was imprisoned at the Doges' Palace for sorcery but made a daring escape one year later, returning to a debauched lifestyle in the capital cities of Europe. After a period in Spain he returned to Venice as a spy for the Inquisition but he was soon forced to flee once more. He spent his remaining years as a librarian for a Bohemian count. He died in 1798.

Above: *Marco Polo*
Right: *Casanova as depicted on a Spanish postcard*

# Top Ten



*Pointed star detail of the floor inside Santa Maria della Salute*

# 1
# Basilica di San Marco

29D2

Piazza San Marco

Oct–end Apr Mon–Sat 9.45–5.30, Sun 2–4; Nov–end Mar Mon–Sat 9.45–4.30, Sun 2–4

Piazza San Marco (€€€)

Vallaresso/San Zaccaria

Poor

Basilica free. Museo Marciano, Treasury and Pala d'Oro inexpensive

Palazzo Ducale (➤ 20), Piazza San Marco (➤ 21), Campanile (➤ 35)

*This is one of the most visited places in Europe and should not be missed—the exotic Byzantine–Venetian basilica is simply one of the world's greatest medieval buildings.*

The cathedral of Venice evokes the blending of East and West that is at the heart of the Venetian character. More oriental than European, the architecture, the decoration and the atmosphere of ancient sanctity span both the centuries and the styles of Mediterranean civilization.

Originally built to house the body of St. Mark, the patron saint of Venice, which had been smuggled from its tomb in Alexandria by Venetians merchants in AD828, the basilica evolved its present appearance between the 9th and 19th centuries. The basic building dates from the late 11th century, the domes from the 13th and the decoration from subsequent centuries. Much of the decoration was plundered or presented to Venice during its time of supremacy, most notably the four famous gilded horses above the main doors. Made in the 4th century AD to surmount a Roman triumphal arch, they were looted from Constantinople, when it was sacked by the Venetians during the Crusades, and stood on the outside for nearly 600 years until plundered, in turn, by the French. After the Napoleonic wars, they were restored to the basilica although, because of atmospheric pollution, the originals are now kept in a gallery inside while replicas stand in their place.

The richness of ornament outside and inside the basilica can occupy hours, but even the hurried visitor can admire the glowing gold of the mosaics that cover nearly half a hectare (1 acre) of the vaulting or examine them more closely from the galleries. If you don't have time to go inside, or the teeming crowds that engulf the Basilica prove too much

*The magnificent interior of the Basilica di San Marco*

for you, spend a few minutes taking in the exterior details. The central door's wonderful Romanesque carvings dating from the 13th century are considered the exterior's greatest treasures. Superbly carved, they show the earth, the seas and animals on the underside, with the virtues and the beatiudes on the outer face and the Zodiac and labours of the month on the inner.

*Mosaic detail on the exterior of the Basilicia*

If you have more time to go inside make sure you see the most famous single treasure of San Marco, the elaborate gold Byzantine altarpiece, the Pala d'Oro. Encrusted with over 2,600 pearls, rubies, emeralds and other precious stones, it was started in the 10th century but was not completed until 1342.

The Basilica has been the cathedral of Venice only since 1807. Before that time it had been the shrine of San Marco and the chapel of the Doge, while the church of San Pietro di Castello in the far east of the city (➤ 55) had been the cathedral, an arrangement to minimize the influence of the Papacy on the affairs of Venice.

# 2
# Canal Grande

 28A4–29C2

 Piazza San Marco

1, 82 (plus 3, 4 in summer)

Good

*This must be one of the best places in the world to take a boat trip. Take in all the city's finest palaces and scenes of Venetian life along the way.*

Following the course of an original creek through the muddy islands of the lagoon, the serpentine canal sweeps in two great curves from what is now the Santa Lucia rail station to the Basin of San Marco. It varies in width from 40–70m (130–230ft), has a maximum depth of 5.5m (18ft) and is crossed by three bridges—the Scalzi, the Rialto and the Accademia—and seven *traghetto* (ferry gondola) routes.

Travelling eastwards along the Canal, some of the principal buildings between the station and the Rialto Bridge are, on the left-hand side, the Scalzi, San Geremia and San Marcuola churches and the palaces Ca' Labia (Tiepolo frescoes), Ca' Vendramin-Calergi (the Municipal Casino in winter) and the Ca' d'Oro (museum and art gallery). On the right-hand side are the San Simeone Piccolo and San Stae churches, the palaces Fondaco dei Turchi (Natural History Museum), Ca' Pesaro (Galleries of Modern Art and Oriental Art) and Ca' Favretto (Hotel San Cassiano)—and then the fish, fruit and vegetable markets just before the Rialto Bridge.

Between the Rialto and the Accademia bridges are, on the left-hand side, the church of San Samuele and the Ca' Mocenigo (where Lord Byron began to write *Don Juan* and not to be confused with the Palazzo Mocenigo, which is open to the public) and Ca' Grassi (at present closed); on the right-hand side, the palace Ca' Rezzonico (museum of 18th-century arts)—then, at the Accademia Bridge, the Accademia Gallery in the former church and *scuola* (school) of Santa Maria della Carità. Between the Accademia Bridge and the Basin of San Marco are, on the left-hand side, Ca' Barbaro (where many artists and writers stayed), Ca' Grande (Prefecture of Police), Ca' Gritti-Pisani (Gritti Palace Hotel), Ca' Tiepolo (Europa e Regina Hotel) and the buildings around Piazza San Marco.

On the right-hand side are the church of Santa Maria della Salute and the palaces of Ca' Venier dei Leoni (the unfinished palace housing the Peggy Guggenheim Collection of Modern Art), Ca' Dario (its façade richly inlaid with multi-coloured marble) and, at the extreme end, the Dogana di Mare (the Customs House), viewable from outside only.

*Waiting for the boat canalside*

# 3

# Gallerie dell'Accademia

*This the initimate home to some of the best of Venetian art spanning the 14th to the 18th centuries, from Byzantine to baroque.*

The most famous and comprehensive collection of Venetian painting is housed in this former church, monastery and *scuola* at the Dorsoduro side of the wooden Accademia Bridge (one of the three crossing points of the Canal Grande). Most paintings come from palaces and churches in the city, and although it would have been more appropriate to see them in their original settings, here they are grouped in galleries and are well lit.

Usually some galleries are closed for various reasons, but there is always enough on display to delight and even sometimes to cause visual and mental indigestion—try to avoid Sundays, which are particularly busy. Highlights include Giovanni Bellini's *Madonna Enthroned* and Carpaccio's *The Presentation of Jesus* in Room II; Giorgione's *Tempest* and Bellini's *Madonna of the Trees* in Room V; Titian's *St. John the Baptist* in Room VI; three magnificent paintings by Veronese in Room XI; the Accademia's only Canaletto and six charming 18th-century *Scenes from Venetian Life* by Longhi in Room XVII; and Carpaccio's enchanting series of paintings illustrating *The Legend of St. Ursula*, portraying the clothes and settings of 15th-century Venice, in Room XXI.

**www.**gallerieaccademia.org

28B2

Campo della Carità, Dorsoduro

041 520 0345

Mon 8.15–2, Tue–Sun 8.15–7.15 (last entrance at 6.30)

Accademia

Poor; some steps

Expensive; a combined ticket for the Accademia, the Ca' d'Oro and Museo Orientale is a good buy

*Popular venue—the entrance to the Galleria dell'Accademia*

# 4
# Palazzo Ducale

*The delicate tracery columns of the Palazzo Ducale*

*The palace, a vast, grandiose civic building, is the cream of Italy's Gothic constructions, with a fairy-tale pink and white exterior.*

Venice was governed from the Doges' Palace for a thousand years, and it still dominates the city. The pink palace, with its white colonnades that can be seen across the water from the Basin of San Marco, looks much as it did when it replaced an earlier building in the 14th century, except that its pillars seem foreshortened because the level of the surrounding pavement has been raised. Here the elected doge of Venice held his court and presided over a system of councils, designed to prevent any one self-interested faction seizing power. Once, when this failed, the over-ambitious Doge Marin Falier was convicted of treason and beheaded at the top of the new marble staircase in the palace courtyard and his portrait replaced by a black cloth, which can still be seen.

Visitors to the palace can marvel at the succession of richly decorated council chambers on the second floor, their walls and ceilings painted by the leading Venetian painters, including Tintoretto, whose *Paradise* is one of the largest old master paintings in the world. It graces the wall of the Sala del Maggior Consiglio (Great Council Chamber), a vast hall designed to seat 1,700 citizens who had the right to vote in the council. Have a look at the Armoury, a collection of some 2,000 weapons and suits of armour.

From the Palace itself, the Ponte dei Sospiri (Bridge of Sighs) crosses a canal to the prison and the notorious, waterlogged dungeons below water level known as *pozzi* (the wells). You can join guided tours through the palace and the prison and also special tours of the 'secret rooms' (in English, French and Italian). This includes the interrogation rooms and torture chamber of the State Inquisitors and the cells under the roof of the prison, called 'the leads', from which Casanova made his dramatic escape in 1756, while serving a five-year sentence on charges involving blasphemy, magic and espionage.

The Doges' Palace is so rich in art and architectural splendours that a whole morning or afternoon could be devoted to it. When Venice is crowded, it is best to arrive early to enjoy an unhurried tour. If you visit in winter be sure to dress warmly as the Palazzo Ducale has no heating and is extremely cold.

**www.**museiciviciveneziani.it

- 29D2
- Piazzetta di San Marco
- 041 520 9070/041 271 5911
- Apr–end Oct daily 9–7; Nov–end Mar daily 9–5
- Café (€–€€)
- Vallaresso/San Zaccaria.
- Poor; steps to upper floors
- Expensive
- Basilica San Marco (► 16–17), Piazza San Marco (► 21), Campanile (► 35)

# 5
# Piazza San Marco

*Visitors do flock here in their thousands and it can be rather daunting, but the scale and spectacle of this piazza is breathtaking.*

The Piazza San Marco is the heart of Venice. When Napoleon conquered the Venetian Republic he called it 'the most elegant drawing-room in Europe', and so it still is. At the eastern end stands the Basilica di San Marco with its Byzantine domes; to one side its campanile, the Piazzetta outside the Doges' Palace and the Basin of San Marco; to the other the Clock Tower and the Piazzetta dei Leoncini, named after the red marble lions standing there. The north side of the Piazza is bounded by the Procuratie Vecchie, the former offices of the Republic's administration, with an arcade of shops below and the Café Quadri, once patronised by the Austrian occupiers of Venice. On the south side is the former administration building, the Procuratie Nuove, with another arcade of shops and the Café Florian, the favourite of Venetian patriots during the Austrian occupation, below. At the western end of the Piazza, the church of San Geminiano was demolished on Napoleon's orders, and a new arcade with a ballroom above was built (the entrance of the Correr Museum of Venetian history is now there, ► 44). The two granite columns near the water's edge in the Piazzetta were set up in the 12th century; one is surmounted by a stone Lion of St. Mark, the other by the figure of St. Theodore, the first patron saint of the city, proudly wielding shield and spear.

29D2

Piazza San Marco

Florian (€–€€€) and Quadri (€–€€€)

Vallaresso/San Marco

Basilica San Marco (► 16–17), Palazzo Ducale (► 20), Campanile (► 35)

*View into Piazza San Marco at night*

# 6
# San Giorgio Maggiore

29D1–E1

Campo San Giorgio, Isola San Giorgio Maggiore

041 522 7827

May–end Sep daily 9.30–12.30, 2.30–6.30; Oct–end Apr daily 9.30–12.30, 2.30–4.30

San Giorgio

None

Church free, campanile moderate

*The cool interior of Palladio's San Giorgio Maggiore*
Below: *A bird's-eye view of San Giorgio Maggiore*

*A tranquil haven from the bustle of San Marco, this magnificent Palladian church has tremendous views from the campanile.*

The church stands on its island across the Basin of San Marco, giving Venice one of its most celebrated views. Designed by Andrea Palladio in the 16th century, it has all the majesty that the term 'Palladian' implies, and this is particularly apparent at night when the dazzling marble façade is floodlit. Originally founded in 790, the first church was destroyed by an earthquake in 1223 and not rebuilt until Palladio began work in 1559, the 1443 monastery next door taking precedence. The result was worth waiting for—one of the finest example's of Italian neoclassical architecture, complete with four-columned portico. Don't miss the choir stalls, which have some of the finest wood carving in Venice.

The interior is vast and austere, its white stone a magnificent setting for its works of art, including paintings by Tintoretto and a bronze altarpiece, *The Globe Surmounted by God the Father*, dating from the 16th century. Other highlights by Tinteretto, splendidly offset by the light from the high windows, are *The Fall of Manna* and *The Last Supper* (both 1592–94), hung in the choir stalls. To the right of the choir stalls in the Cappela dei Morti is hung what may be Tintoretto's last work, *The Deposition* (1594).

The tall and slender campanile, ascended by a lift, offers the best bird's-eye views of Venice because, unlike that of San Marco, it is detached from the city and can therefore be seen as a panorama across the water.

# 7 Santa Maria Gloriosa dei Frari

*Another superb Gothic building and Venice's second largest church, it is filled with magnificent paintings, monuments and ornate woodwork.*

This church is Venice's second largest and has some impressive statistics. Built of brick it is huge, 98m (322ft) long, 46m (151ft) wide and 28m (92ft) high and dates from the 14th and 15th centuries. Reached through a maze of streets, it was the Franciscans' Venetian powerbase, originally founded in 1250. The church stands on the far side of the Canal Grande and is almost as large as Santi Giovanni e Paolo but has a wholly different character. The choir screen and stalls remain in place and the nave is shadowed and sombre, as are the vast and elaborate monuments. Memorable among these is the open-doored vast white pyramid (1827) containing the heart of the 19th-century sculptor Antonio Canova. He designed it as a monument to the great Venetian painter Titian (*d*1576), who, in fact, is buried across the aisle under a dramatic 19th-century statue.

Two paintings are the particular glories of the Frari. One is Titian's huge *The Assumption* (1516–18), still in the position for which it was painted above the high altar. The other is *The Madonna and Child* by Bellini in the sacristy, one of the loveliest paintings in Venice.

Like Santi Giovanni e Paolo (► 25) the Frari can easily occupy an hour or more for those with a particular interest in painting, sculpture and architecture.

**www**.basilicadeifrari.it

28B3

Campo dei Frari, San Polo

041 522 2637/041 275 0494

Mon–Sat 9–6, Sun 1–6

San Tomà

Good; one or two steps

Inexpensive

Gallerie dell'Accademia (► 19), Scoula Grande di San Roco (► 26)

*Santa Maria Gloriosa dei Frari displays fine paintings*

# 8
# Santa Maria della Salute

29C2

Campo della Salute, Dorsoduro, near the eastern end of the Grand Canal

041 522 5558

Apr–end Sep daily 9–12, 3–6.30; Oct–end Mar daily 9–12, 3–5.30. Sacristy Mon–Sat 10–11.30, 3–5, Sun 3–5

Salute

Poor; several steps

Church free; sacristy inexpensive

*This great baroque church stands proudly at the entrance to the Grand Canal, one of the most imposing landmarks in the city*

Like the Redentore (➤ 50) this church was built to give thanks for the ending of a plague but in the following century. The great domed church has sometimes been seen as the hostess of the city, welcoming visitors; as the novelist Henry James wrote: 'like some great lady on the threshold of her salon...with her domes and scrolls, her scalloped buttresses and statues forming a pompous crown, and her wide steps disposed on the ground like the train of a robe'. After dark, a walk through the alleys of Dorsoduro can suddenly end on the brilliantly floodlit steps of the Salute beneath its gleaming bulk, the water below dancing with reflected light.

The magnificent baroque interior is more restrained and somewhat austure in comparision to the exuberant exterior. You can view an early Titian, *The Descent of the Holy Spirit* (1550), third on the left. Other fine paintings can be found in the sacristy, with eight more Titians and Tinteretto's magnificent *Marriage Feast at Cana* (1561). Look for his self-portrait—the artist is depicted as the first Apostle on the left. You have to pay an admission charge to see these paintings, but it's worth it.

Venetians still come to the church on 21st November, the feast day of the Salute, to give thanks for good health.

*Illuminated at night—Santa Maria della Salute*

# 9
# Santi Giovanni e Paolo

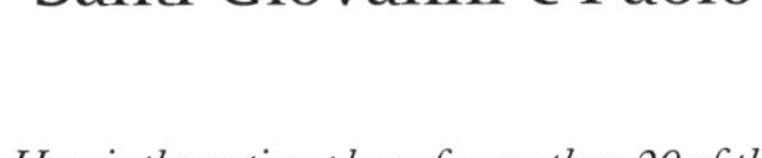

*Here is the resting place of more than 20 of the city's doges, buried beneath monumental tombs within a majestic Gothic church.*

Called San Zanipolo by Venetians, the church stands to the north of San Marco. The largest church in Venice, it measures 101m (331ft) in length, is 38m (125ft) wide and 33m (108ft) high and was built by the Dominicans in the 14th and 15th centuries. Despite its bulk, the red brick building is not ponderous, partly because of the cleaning of the elaborate Gothic portals at the west end and the monuments within. It is best seen on a sunny day as the interior can be dark on a dull day.

Inside, the original choir screen and stalls have not survived, leaving the nave light and airy. The church is commonly called the Pantheon of Doges, and around the walls stand magnificent monuments to doges and, amongst other notables, the Venetian general Marcantonio Bragadin, who was flayed alive by the Turks when they captured Cyprus in 1571. Not only does a fresco on the monument depict this, but the flayed skin, which was stolen from Constantinople, lies in a small sarcophagus. His death was avenged at the Battle of Lepanto by Doge Sebastiano Venier, whose fine bronze statue also stands in the church.

29D3

Campo Santi Giovanni e Paolo, Castello

041 523 5913

Mon–Sat 7.30–7, Sun 3–6

Rosa Salva bar for coffee nearby (€)

Fondamenta Nove/Ospedale Civile

Good; one step

Inexpensive

Santa Maria dei Miracoli (► 62)

*View across the city from the top of the Campanile de San Marco to Santi Gionvanni e Paolo*

# 10
# Scoula Grande di San Rocco

www.scuolagrandesnroccco.it

28B3

Campo San Rocco, San Polo

041 523 4864

Apr–end Oct daily 9–5.30; Nov–end Mar daily 9–4

San Tomà

Poor

Moderate

Santa Maria Gloriosa dei Friari (► 23), Scuola Grande dei Carmini (► 65)

*Drawn in by the mastery of the cycle of 54 paintings by Tinteretto, you won't be disappointed by the stunning ornate interior.*

This is the largest and grandest of the *scuole*, standing close to the church of the Frari. It was founded in honour of St. Roch, a saint who dedicated his life to the care of the sick. It is most celebrated for its great series of powerful paintings by Tintoretto depicting Biblical scenes, a monumental achievement covering the walls and ceilings of this magnificent *scoula*. It is best to start by heading up the great staircase to the Sala dell'Albergo, off the main hall, to see the works in the order Tintoretto painted them. The room is dominated by the powerful *Crucifixion* (1565), one of the greatest paintings in the world. In the main upper hall you will find striking ceiling paintings depicting scenes from the Old Testament. The vast scenes on the walls depict episodes from the New Testament, showing his departure from contemporary ideas with wonderful use of colour, form and light.

Coming back downstairs to the Ground Floor Hall you will find the final paintings in Tinteretto's cycle, a culmination of 23 years of work. Here the artist is at his most sublime, as seen in the execution of the *Annunciation* and the *Flight into Egypt*. These reflect the artist's late style, and the use of dramatic light is revolutionary for its time. In addition to these superb paintings and ornate interior, look for the beautiful carvings below the paintings, works by 17th-century sculptor Francesco Pianta.

*The striking white façade of the Scoula Grande di San Rocco*

# What To See



*Madonna mosaic on a Venetian building*

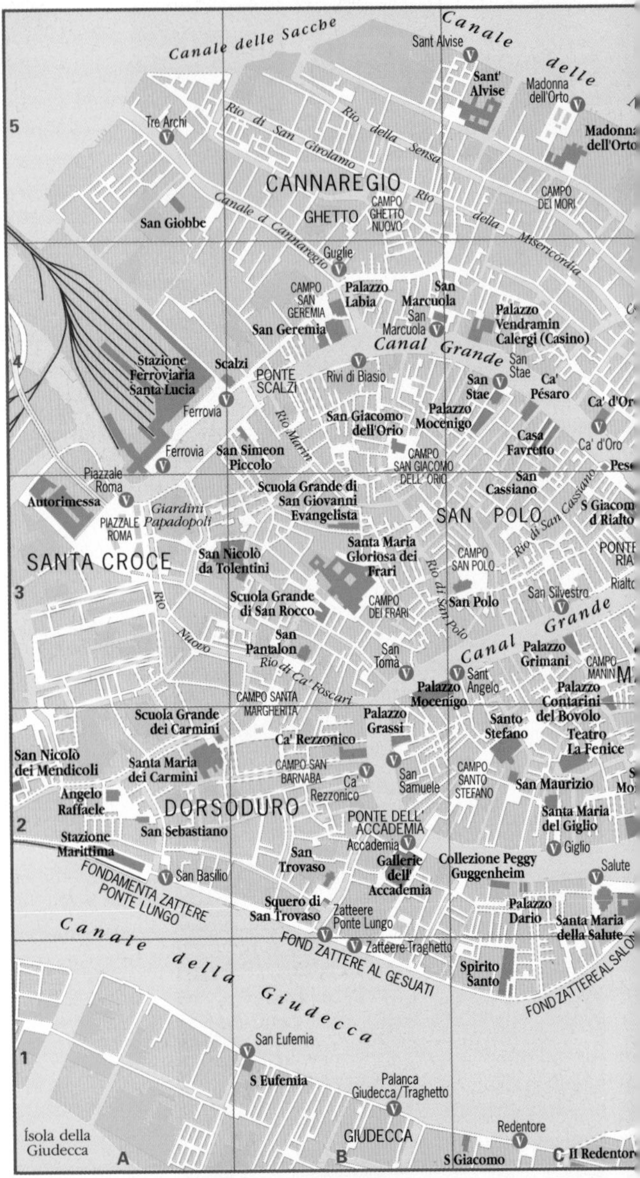

Canale delle Sacche
Canale delle
Sant Alvise
Sant' Alvise
Madonna dell'Orto
Madonna dell'Orto
5
Tre Archi
Rio di San Girolamo
Rio della Sensa
CANNAREGIO
CAMPO GHETTO NUOVO
GHETTO
Rio della Misericordia
CAMPO DEI MORI
San Giobbe
Canale di Cannaregio
Guglie
CAMPO SAN GEREMIA
Palazzo Labia
San Marcuola
San Marcuola
Palazzo Vendramin Calergi (Casino)
San Geremia
Canal Grande
4
Stazione Ferroviaria Santa Lucia
Scalzi
PONTE SCALZI
Rivi di Biasio
San Stae
San Stae
Ca' Pésaro
Ca' d'Oro
Ferrovia
Rio Marin
San Giacomo dell'Orio
Palazzo Mocenigo
Casa Favretto
Ca' d'Oro
Ferrovia
San Simeon Piccolo
CAMPO SAN GIACOMO DELL' ORIO
Pesc
Piazzale Roma
Scuola Grande di San Giovanni Evangelista
San Cassiano
Autorimessa
Giardini Papadopoli
PIAZZALE ROMA
SAN POLO
Rio di San Cassiano
S Giacom d Rialto
Santa Maria Gloriosa dei Frari
SANTA CROCE
San Nicolò da Tolentini
CAMPO SAN POLO
PONTE RIA
Rialto
3
Rio Nuovo
Scuola Grande di San Rocco
CAMPO DEI FRARI
Rio di San Polo
San Polo
San Silvestro
Canal Grande
San Pantalon
San Tomà
Palazzo Grimani
CAMPO MANIN
Rio di Ca' Foscari
Sant Angelo
Palazzo Mocenigo
Palazzo Contarini del Bovolo
CAMPO SANTA MARGHERITA
Scuola Grande dei Carmini
Palazzo Grassi
Santo Stefano
Teatro La Fenice
Ca' Rezzonico
San Nicolò dei Mendicoli
Santa Maria dei Carmini
CAMPO SAN BARNABA
Ca' Rezzonico
San Samuele
CAMPO SANTO STEFANO
San Maurizio
Angelo Raffaele
DORSODURO
PONTE DELL' ACCADEMIA
Santa Maria del Giglio
2
Stazione Marittima
San Sebastiano
Accademia
Giglio
San Trovaso
Gallerie dell' Accademia
Collezione Peggy Guggenheim
Salute
FONDAMENTA ZATTERE PONTE LUNGO
San Basilio
Squero di San Trovaso
Zatteere Ponte Lungo
Palazzo Dario
Santa Maria della Salute
Canale della Giudecca
FOND ZATTERE AL GESUATI
Zatteere-Traghetto
Spirito Santo
FOND ZATTERE AL SALON
San Eufemia
1
S Eufemia
Palanca Giudecca/Traghetto
Ísola della Giudecca
GIUDECCA
Redentore
A
B
S Giacomo
C
Il Redentore

# VENICE

100 200 300 400 m

San Michele
Cimitero
Cimitero
Ísola di San Michele
Canale delle Fondamenta Nuove
Gesuiti
Fondamente Nuove
Rio dei Gesuiti
Santi Apostoli
Rio dei Mendicanti
Ospedale Civile
Santa Maria dei Miracoli
Scuola di San Marco
Santi Giovanni e Paolo
San Giovanni Crisostomo
CAMPO SANTI GIOVANNI E PAOLO
Rio d Santa Giustina
Celestia
San Francesco della Vigna
Bacini
CAMPO SANTA MARIA FORMOSA
Santa Maria della Fava
Santa Maria Formosa
Palazzo Querini-Stampalia
Scuola di San Giórgio degli Schiavoni
San Salvador
Rio d Pietà
CASTELLO
Museo Diocesano d'Arte Sacra
San Giórgio dei Greci
Torre dell'Orologio
Basilica di San Marco
CAMPO BANDLERA E MORO
Arsenale
PIAZZA SAN MARCO
Campanile
San Zaccaria
Palazzo Ducale (Doge's Palace)
La Pietà
San Giovanni in Brágora
San Martino
Caffè Florian
San Zaccaria
RIVA DEGLI SCHIAVONI
Museo Stórico Navale
San Marco
Arsenale
Vallaresso
Punta della Dogana
Canale di San Marco
San Giorgio
San Giorgio Maggiore
Giardini
Giardini Pubblici
Zitelle
Zitelle
Ísola di San Giorgio Maggiore
D
E
F

# Venice

One of the most painted, filmed and written about cities in the world, Venice is disturbingly beautiful; nothing quite prepares you for that first glimpse of distant domes and spires emerging from the flat, grey waters like a mirage. Or on a sunny day when the water sparkles like a thousand tiny lanterns, its magic is breathtaking. Within the city, murky canal water laps the bases of dreamlike buildings, creating a slightly disorienting, rocking effect enhanced by the gentle rattle of the wind as it brushes against the boats and mooring poles. Behind the canals lie tiny, winding alleys in which even the best map reader soon gets lost and all sense of urgency has to be forgotten. Time is irrelevant; this place weaves its spell and lingers in the memory until the next visit releases another onslaught on the senses.

*‘White phantom city, whose untrodden streets, Are rivers, and whose pavements are the shifting Shadows of the palaces and strips of sky’*

HENRY WADSWORTH LONGFELLOW
*Venice* (1876)

*Boats moored in the Santa Barnaba district of the city*

# The City of Venice

**The city is divided into six *sestieri* (districts): to the north and east of the Grand Canal San Marco is in the centre, with Castello to the east; to the south and west Dorsoduro lies across the Grand Canal from San Marco with the workaday areas of San Polo, then Santa Croce and finally Cannaregio to the north. The aquatic highway by which most of the *sestieri* are reached is the main street of the city and that is, of course, the Grand Canal.**

Each area has its own points of interest and individual character. The most expensive area to stay and eat out in is around San Marco. This district and the streets leading to the Rialto Bridge and along the waterfront can get very busy at times. The streets of central Venice are very narrow and quite often finish in a dead end. Without a good map it is easy to get disorientated, although it adds to the fun. For a more relaxed and cheaper option Dosoduro, with its fine churches and picturesque squares, is a good bet. Many people choose to stay towards Castello, which offers some cheaper pensiones (small hotel) and restaurants.

*Dining by the canal in the San Marco district*

# What to See in Venice

## ANGELO RAFFAELE ✪

This church, one of the city's oldest foundations, is located in a secluded part of Dorsoduro. It is notable for its 18th-century organ decorated with paintings by Guardi.

- 28A5
- Campo Angelo Raffaele
- 041 522 8548
- Daily 9–12, 3–5
- San Basilio · Free

## ARSENALE ✪

The naval powerhouse of the Venetian Empire was the Arsenale, the great dockyard in the east of the city. Surrounded by 15th-century castellated walls and entered through a monumental archway and watergate, it was where the galleys that conquered the Mediterranean and dominated it for centuries were built and based. The interior is now mostly deserted dockside and bare walls, but the gates—guarded by stone lions brought from Greece in the 17th and 18th centuries—can easily be admired from the campo (square) outside.

- 29E2
- Campiello della Malvasia
- Arsenale
- Moderate

Above: *Detail on the pulpit in the church of Angelo Raffale*

## BASILICA DI SAN MARCO (► 16–17, TOP TEN)

## CA' D'ORO ✪✪

The 'House of Gold', the most famous palazzo on the Grand Canal, was named after the gilding on its elaborate exterior when it was new. Inside the palazzo an elegant new gallery displays Italian art, including frescoes by Titian and Giorgione. Reopened in 1984, this magnificent building retains its architectural bones, but sadly not its atmosphere of former grandeur. You can get a really good view of the palazzo from the opposite side of the Grand Canal at the Pescheria (fish market).

**www.**cadoro.org

- 28C4
- Grand Canal, Cannaregio
- 041 523 8790
- Mon 8.15–2, Tue–Sun 8.15–7.15
- Ca' d'Oro
- Moderate
- Santi Giovanni e Paolo (► 25), Santa Maria dei Miracoli (► 62)

www.caffeflorian.com
29D2
Piazza San Marco 56
041 520 5641
May–end Oct daily 9.30am–midnight; Nov–end Apr Thu–Tue 9.30am–midnight
Vallaresso (San Marco)
Basilica di San Marco (► 16–17), Palazzo Ducale (► 20), Campanile di San Marco (► 35)

**CAFFÈ FLORIAN** ✪✪

This charming, frescoed café has been in business since 1720 and serves some of the most expensive coffee and hot chocolate in the city. But how could you resist sitting at an outside table in the very heart and soul of the city, the Piazza di San Marco. When established by Floriano Francesoni it was known as Venezia Trionfante and by the early 1800s was a Venetian favourite, favoured by Lord Byron and German poet Goethe.

**CANAL GRANDE (► 18, TOP TEN)**

www.museiciviciveneziani.it
28C4
Canal Grande, Santa Croce
Palace and museums 041 524 0662
Palace and museums Apr–end Oct Tue–Sun 10–6; Nov–end Mar Tue–Sun 10–5
San Stae
Moderate, includes admission to palace and museums

**CA' PESARO GALLERIA D' ARTE MODERNA E MUSEO ORIENTALE** ✪✪✪

Worth visiting if only to see inside this enormous 17th-century restored baroque palazzo overlooking the Grand Canal. It was built for Giovanni Pesaro, who became Doge in 1658. It houses contemporary art exhibitions on the first two floors and Oriental art on the top floor.

The Museo Orientale has a wealth of artefacts collected by Conti di Bardi during a lengthy voyage to the Far East in the 19th century. The Museo d'Arte Moderna was founded in 1902 with a handful of pedestrian pieces bought from the Biennale however, it does now contain works by such artists as Matisse, Miró and Klee.

## CA' REZZONICO MUSEO DELL SETTECENTO VENEZIANO (MUSEUM OF 18TH-CENTURY VENICE) ✪✪✪

This immensely grand 17th-century palace overlooking the Grand Canal has been filled with furniture and paintings of the 18th century. The magnificent rooms of the piano nobile (main floor) are richly decorated with gilding, frescoes and painted ceilings, including one by Tiepolo. On the floor above you can see paintings of Venetian life by Guardi and Longhi as well as a succession of small rooms, decorated with frescoes by the younger Tiepolo. The top floor, which houses a collection of costumes, the stock of a pharmacist's shop and a marionette theatre, is often closed.

The poet Robert Browning occupied a suite of rooms below the piano nobile (not open to the public) from 1888 until his death here in 1889.

www.museicivicivenezianí.it
28B2
Canal Grande, Dorsoduro
041 241 0100
Apr–end Oct Wed–Mon 10–6; Nov–end Mar Wed–Mon 10–5
Ca' Rezzonico
Expensive
Gallerie dell'Accademia (► 19), Santa Maria Gloriosa dei Frari (► 23), Scoula Grande di San Rocco (► 26), Scoula Grande dei Carmini (► 65)

## CAMPANILE DI SAN MARCO ✪✪✪

The bell tower rises 99m (325ft) above the piazza, the tallest building in Venice. The original collapsed in 1902 in a heap of rubble but was rebuilt over the next 10 years. It is entered through the beautiful little loggetta, built in the 16th century by Jacopo Sansovino and restored after it was destroyed in 1902. An internal lift takes visitors to the gallery surrounding the belfry, which commands panoramic views of the city, the lagoon and, on clear days, the Veneto and the Alps.

29D2
Piazza San Marco
041 522 4064
Jul–end Aug daily 9–9; Apr–end Jun, Sep, Oct daily 9–7; Nov–end Mar daily 9.30–4.15
San Zaccaria/Vallaresso (San Marco)
Expensive
Basilica di San Marco (► 16–17), Palazzo Ducale (► 20), Piazza San Marco (► 21)

## CAMPO DEI MORI ✪✪

This is one of the quieter squares in the city, off the tourist trail in Cannaregio, and a lovely spot for an ice cream, a coffee or a drink in one of the little friendly bars. You can mingle with the locals and watch the world go by. It is also close to two of the finest churches in the city, Sant'Alvise (► 59) and Madonna dell'Orto (► 43). It gives you an insight into real Venetian street life, away from the masses.

28C5
Orto

*Moorish statue on Tintoretto's house in the Campo dei Mori*

28B2
Ca' Rezzonico

Below: *First communion—in the Campo Santa Maria Formosa*
Opposite top: *Pausing in Campo Santo Stefano*
Opposite below: *Dogna di Mare*

## CAMPO SAN BARNABA ✪✪

Perhaps the most charmingly Venetian of all the squares is the Campo San Barnaba near the Accademia Gallery. Presided over by the noble façade of the church of San Barnaba (a simple parish church with an air of tranquillity) this bustles with life: shops, two cafés with tables outside and a barge selling the world's most photographed fruit and vegetables moored in the canal that connects with the Grand Canal.

28C3
San Silvestro

## CAMPO SAN POLO 

On the other side of the Grand Canal, the largest square is Campo San Polo, where the huge marble wellhead is a gathering place for the young on summer evenings.

28B3
Ca' Rezzonico

## CAMPO SANTA MARGHERITA 

More lively is the Campo Santa Margherita, where vendors sell fruit, vegetables, fish and shoes, and local Venetian life goes on undisturbed by crowds of tourists.

29D3
San Zaccaria/Rialto

## CAMPO SANTA MARIA FORMOSA ✪

Campo Santa Maria Formosa, around the church of that name (► 60), is busy with market stalls and open-air café tables. An eclectic mix of homelike and palatial buildings.

29D3
Fondamenta Nove/ Ospedale

## CAMPO SANTI GIOVANNI E PAOLO 

On the San Marco side of the Grand Canal this square in front of the huge church of Santi Giovanni e Paolo (► 25), is dominated by the remarkable equestrian bronze statue of Bartolomeo Colleoni, a famous Venetian general of the 15th century.

**CAMPO SANTO STEFANO** ✪

This is one of Venice's finest squares, busy and popular but big enough to abosrb the crowds, the local children, the students and backpackers who meet up here. At its north end is the church of Santo Stefano (► 64), one of the city's lovliest. There are some good cafés, with the best known Paolin (► 98), said to serve the best ice cream in Venice. When you relax here it can be difficult to visualize it as a former bullfighting arena, where oxen were tied to stakes and were baited by dogs, a practice abandoned in 1802.

- 28C2
- Accademia

**COLLEZIONE PEGGY GUGGENHEIM** ✪✪✪

The collection of Cubist, Abstract and Surrealist art acquired by the late Peggy Guggenheim, the American millionairess, is housed in her former home, an unfinished 18th-century palazzo on the Canal Grande, Palazzo Venier de Leoni. This is the perfect antidote to a superfluity of Byzantine, Gothic Renaissance and baroque art. Paintings and sculptures of the 20th century—including Peggy Guggenheim's own discovery, the energetic Jackson Pollock—will delight those who appreciate modern art, while those who do not will enjoy the view from the garden, overlooking the Grand Canal. This is one of the world's most important 20th-century collections outside the US.

www.guggenheim-venice.it

- 28C2
- Calle San Cristoforo, Dorsoduro
- 041 240 5411
- Apr–end Oct Wed–Mon 10–6, Sat 10–10; Nov–end Mar Wed–Mon 10–6
- Accademia/ Salute
- Expensive
- Gallerie dell'Accademia (► 19), Santa Maria della Salute (► 24), Ca' Rezzonica (► 35)

**DOGANA DI MARE (CUSTOMS HOUSE)** ✪✪

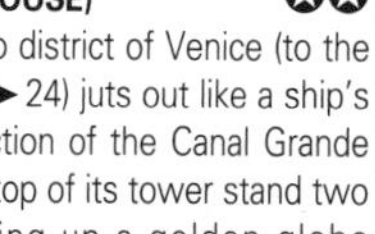

This stands where the Dorsoduro district of Venice (to the east of the church of the Salute ► 24) juts out like a ship's prow into the lagoon at the junction of the Canal Grande and the Basin of San Marco. On top of its tower stand two bronze figures of Atlas holding up a golden globe surmounted by a figure of Fortune as a wind vane. Behind the tower are the 17th-century Customs warehouses. You can stop for a moment and enjoy the views to San Marco and over the lagoon.

- 28C2
- Dosoduro
- closed to public except during exhibitions
- Salute

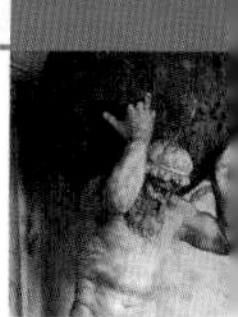

## GALLERIE DELL'ACCADEMIA (➤ 19, TOP TEN)

## GHETTO ✪✪✪

This a small district enclosed by canals in the northwest of the city and not far from the rail station. It was named after a 14th-century cannon-casting foundry, or *geto* in Venetian—the name was subsequently given to Jewish enclaves the world over. Since Jews were only permitted to live in this small area from 1516 to 1797, they were allowed to build higher houses than elsewhere in the city and so they rise to eight floors.

The main approach to the Ghetto is through a narrow alley leading off the Fondamenta di Cannaregio. This brings you to the Ghetto Vecchio and over a bridge to the Campo Ghetto Nuovo, a separate island that's the heart of the Ghetto and where you will find the the Holocaust Memorial, a series of seven reliefs by Arbit Blatas, commemorating the deportation and extermination of the city's Jews, and the **Museo Ebraico**. The museum was opened in 1955 and displays a collection of religious objects, prayer books, textiles, documents and silverware.

Today the area remains the focus for the religion, and there are still a small number of Jewish families living in the Ghetto, with two synagogues in regular use and shops selling Jewish books and souvenirs.

**www.**ghetto.it
28B5
Guglie

**Museo Ebraico**
Campo del Ghetto Nuovo
041 715 359
Jun–end Sep Sun–Fri 10–7, Oct–end May Sun–Fri 10–6. May close early on Fri
Moderate

Opposite: *Washing drying in the Castello district*
Below: *The Memorial to the Holocaust in the Campo Ghetto Novo*

# In the Know

If you only have a short time to visit Venice, or would like to get a real flavour of the city, here are some ideas:

## 10 Ways To Be A Local

**Take a pride in the city.** You won't find much litter and there's little cause for police presence.

**Get dressed up for the theatre.** The superb newly restored Teatro La Fenice is the perfect venue for that new outfit.

**Enter into the spirit of Carnevale.** Only reintroduced in 1979, this is when Ventians really let their hair down.

**Learn a few words of Italian.** Even if it's only the basic courtesies, it always goes down well.

**Always carry sunglasses.** It's not just for posing, the sun can be very strong especially reflected off the water, even in winter.

**Take to the beach.** If you really do need to be here in July or August join the locals at the weekend on the Lido or the islands.

**Relax in a park.** It's not just tourists who seek refuge in a park.

**Use bars.** Take a quick coffee standing at the counter or a leisurely cappuccino at an outside table in the campo.

**Try a Bellini.** This cocktail was made famous in Harry's Bar (► 114) and really should be tried.

**Get an early night.** It may sound dull but Venetians don't stay out late and can be home by 10pm.

## 10 Good Places To Have Lunch

**Ai Corazzerie (€–€€)**
Get away from the crowds at this pleasant trattoria and pizzeria with an outside conservatory.
✉ Salizzada dei Corazzierei, Castello 3839
☎ 041 528 9859

**Al Bacco (€€)**
If it's a sunny day take advantage of the pretty courtyard garden at this locals' haunt with great fish and seafood.
✉ Fondamenta Capuzine, Cannaregio 3054 ☎ 041 717 493

**Al Bottegon (€)**
This is one of the best places to have lunch. Snack on excellent panini, washed down by great wine and while you linger catch up on your people watching.
✉ Fondementa Nani, Dorsoduro 992 ☎ 041 523 0034

**Alla Maddelena (€€)**
Lovely island setting for a tasty lunch; the perfect antidote to the busy city. Try the tasty duck.
✉ Mazzorbo 7c ☎ 041 523 6084

**Busa alla Torre (€€)**
When you've bought the glass take a break in this Murano restaurant renowned for its fish.
✉ Campo Santo Stefano, Murano 3 ☎ 041 739 662

**Il Refolo (€€)**
Pleasantly situated by a quiet canal, this is a popular spot for a lunch of pizza, pasta or salad. Good house wine and scrumptious desserts.
✉ Campo San Giacomo dell'Olio, Santa Croce 1459
☎ 041 524 0016

**Locanda Cipriani (€€€)**
You will need a fat wallet to eat here, but it is a gorgeous place to have lunch in the walled garden on the island of Torcello. Superb food.
✉ Piazza Santa Fosca, Torcello 29 ☎ 041 730 150

**Mistra (€–€€)**
On the island of Guidecca in a converted warehouse. Great views over the lagoon here and good fish and seafood dishes.
✉ Fontadementa San Giacomo, Guidecca
☎ 041 522 0743

**Nico (€)**
Must be one of the nicest places to pause and enjoy possibly the best ice cream in the city—right on the watefront. Also sells snacks.
✉ Fondamenta Zattere, Dorsoduro ☎ 041 522 5293

**Vecio Fritolin (€)**
You can have a snack lunch here, very much a local trattoria with a lovely atmosphere. Or you can go the whole hog with a full meal of flame grilled fish. ✉ Calle della Regina, Santa Croce 2262 ☎ 041 522 2281

10

## Best Views

**Arriving**—by water taxi or vaporetto from the airport; it is the perfect way to get your first glimpse of Venice.
**Campanile**—Venice's highest building commands great views of the city and the lagoon (► 35).
**Fondamenta Nuove**—come here to get a fine aspect of the city skyline from the lagoon.
**From a boat on the Grand Canal**—surely the best way to see the beautiful palazzi of Venice.
**Guidecca**—the silhouetted buildings of the Dorsoduro look wonderful from the Campo del Redentore on the island of Guidecca.
**Island of San Giorgio Maggiore**—the best place to get a view of the city is from the campanile of the church (► 22).
**Ponte dell'Accadmia**—terrifice views down the Grand Canal and also towards the church of Santa Maria della Salute (► 24).
**Ponte di Rialto**—just the place to get the a bird's-eye view of the life on the Grand Canal.
**Punta della Dogana**—at this vantage point in Dorsoduro you get a fine view across the mouth of the Grand Canal to the north and the Canale della Guidecca to the south.

**Torcello**—climb the bell tower of the cathedral of Santa Maria Assunta for wonderful lagoon views.

## Best Façades

**Basilica di San Marco** with its fince mosaics and rich ornamentation (► 16–17).
**Ca' d'Oro** may not be as spectacular as it once was but it still impresses (► 33).
**Madonna dell'Orto** has a graceful red-brick and marble Gothic façade (► 43).
**Palazzo Ducale** is an amazing pink palace with white colonnades presiding regally over Piazza San Marco (► 20).
**San Girogio Maggiore** cannot fail to dazzle with its stunning marble exterior (► 22).

## Prettiest Squares

**Santa Barnaba** (► 36).
**Campo San Polo** (► 36)
**Campo Santa Margherita** (► 36).
**Campo Santa Maria Formosa** (► 36)
**Campo Santo Stefano** (► 36)

## Best Souvenirs

**Carnival masks**
**Murano Glass**
**Replica gondolas**
**Paper products**
**Italian food**— pastas, olive oils and traditional Venetian biscuits.

Opposite: *Masks make a good present to take home*
Left:: *Torcello—check out th view from the bell tower*

## GIARDINI PUBBLICCA

29F1
Giardini
Free

On the city's eastern fringes in Castello, this garden is a welcome green space after a heavy dose of architectural grandeur. It was created by Napoleon, who oversaw the draining of a stretch of marshland and the demolition of several convents to generate this shady haven. It is good for a break from the crowds and pleasant for a picnic. You may notice the pavilions partly hidden by the trees, used in the Biennale (➤ 116), the biennual art and film exhibition held from June to September, but these are closed to the public except during the Biennale. The rest is a good grassy space dotted with pine trees and benches, with wide views over the lagoon.

## LA GIUDECCA

28A1–29D1
Palanca/Redentore/Zitelle

The island of the Giudecca lies to the south of central Venice across the wide, deep water Canale della Giudecca. Originally a chain of small islands, it was settled by a small Jewish community, who lived here until the establishment of the Ghetto (➤ 39). It has always been a popular place to escape the summer heat, even as early as the 13th century when wealthy aristocrats built splendid palaces surrounded by gardens. Subsequently in the 19th and 20th centuries it became an industralized area with the creation of factories and shipyards. This has declined over the last 50 years and today it is primarily a residential area. The main sights are on the north side of the island, including the Redentore (➤ 50), the Zittelle and Santa Eufemia churches. Here you will also find bars and restaurants, food shops and examples of 14th-century palazzi.

*View across Giudecca Canal from Zattere to Island of Giudecca*

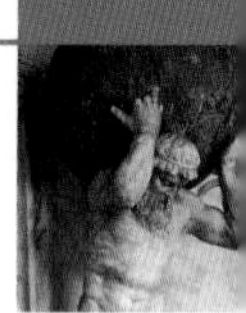

## MADONNA DELL'ORTO ✪✪✪

Isolated in the north of the city in Cannaregio, the church is a good goal for a long walk. A huge, light, airy church reminiscent of Santi Giovanni e Paolo (► 25), it was magnificently restored after the flood of 1966 by funds raised in Britain. Spend a few minutes to admire the mainly Gothic façade before entering the church. The windows are obviously Gothic, the onion-shaped dome echoes the earlier Byzantine style, while the elegant doorway is clearly Renaissance.

The simple interior, with its sense of space, height and light, is laid out in basilica form. Tintoretto, who is buried in one of the side chapels—you can see his tomb—was a parishioner and painted a number of superb pictures as a gift to the church. In the chancel are the magnificent *Last Judgement* and *The Making of the Golden Calf.* Look for the charming *Presentation of the Virgin* located at the end of the right nave above the door. In the apse there are further paintings by Tintoretto, the *Beheading of St. Paul* and *St. Peter's Vision of the Cross,* full of movement and pathos. Other great works include Cima da Conegliano's *St. John the Baptist.*

The church gained its name from the story of a statue of the Madonna and Child found in a local vegetable garden or *orto*, and believed to have worked miracles. The statue can be seen in the Cappella di San Mauro off the end of the right aisle near the main altar.

- 28C5
- Campo Madonna dell'Orto, Cannaregio
- 041 719 933
- Mon–Sat 10–5, Sun 1–5; closed Sun in Jul & Aug
- Orto
- Inexpensive

*Statues along the roof of Madonna dell'Orto*

## MERCATO DI RIALTO ✪✪

The oldest market in the Rialto is the fish market, located on the same site for over 1,000 years. Today it is housed in and around the lovely vaulted neo-Gothic Pescheria. Get here early before the crowds for the best atmosphere. Next to this is an array of fruit and vegetable stalls. The produce may have been shipped from the mainland, but its quality and taste are second to none. The prices are pretty good, too. The original traders and merchants lived in the warren of streets around here, which are bursting with butchers, bakers and purveyors of all kinds of foods.

- 29D3
- Rialto
- Mon–Sat 8–1; fish market is closd on Mon
- Rialto

## MUSEO CIVICO CORRER ✪✪✪

**www.**museicivicivenezianni.it
- 29D2
- Ala Napoleonica, Piazza San Marco
- 041 240 5211 or call centre 041 520 9070
- Apr–end Oct daily 9–7; Nov–end Mar daily 9–5
- Vallaresso (San Marco)
- Expensive but valid for Correr Museo Archeologico, Bilbioteca Marciana and Palazzo Ducale
- Basilica di San Marco (► 16–17), Palazzo Ducale (► 20), Piazza San Marco (► 21) Campanile (► 35)

The principal historical museum of the city runs above the Procuratie Nuove arcade on the west and south sides of the Piazza and is entered by a wide marble staircase at the western end. The museum is based on the 18th-century collection of Teodoro Correr, a Venetian worthy. The exhibits include superb paintings—with some exceptional works by the Bellini family—models, costumes, footwear, books, weapons and armour, much of it captured from the Turks. Particularly sinister is the lion's mask *bocca di leone* (letter/mailbox) for written denunciations of enemies of the state. There are also relics of the Bucintoro, the huge, elaborate ceremonial galley used by the doges. On the first floor you will find the striking statues by Antonio Canova (1757–1822), his technique and mastery one of the finest of his age. The focal point is the poignant study of Deaedalus and Icarus, showing the father fixing wings onto his son's arms.

The Correr is part of an ensemble of linked buildings at the western end of San Marco, which also house the city's archaelogical collections and the Biblioteca Marciana, creating one of Venice's biggest and finest museum complexes. The wonderfully stunning state rooms of the library display manuscripts and early books beneath the ceiling of allergorical Mannerist paintings.

*A portrait of Doge Giovani Mocenigo by Gentile Bellini on display in the Museo Civico Correr*

## MUSEO DIOSCESANO DI ARTE SACRE ✪

- 29D3
- Sant'Apollonia, Castello
- 041 277 0561
- Mon–Sat 10.30–12.30
- San Zaccaria
- Free

This tiny but extraordinary museum is a storeroom and restoration centre for works of art from local churches and monasteries. Some are stolen works of art that have been retrieved by the police. It makes for an ever-changing and pleasantly interesting display of sculpture, silverware and other work, with changing exhibitions in the upstairs gallery. The building dates from the 12th–13th centuries and the museum's main draw is its superb Romanesque cloister, once the focal point of the Benedictine monastery of Sant'Apollonia, the only cloister of this period in the city and a gloriously tranquil place to visit.

*The grand staircase of the Palazzo Contarini de Bovolo is visible from outside*

**MUSEO DELLA FONDAZIONE QUERINI STAMPALIA** ✪

The Querini Stampalia palazzo was the home of another grand Venetian family and 20 rooms are still furnished with their splendid collection of pictures and furniture. Accumulated by aristocrat Giovanni Querini in the 19th century, his foundation specified the opening of a library to promote learning, and it is still used enthusiastically by students today. This and the Palazzo Mocenigo (► 46) are two of many such palaces illustrating the extraordinary richness of Venice at the height of its power.

**www.**querinistampalia.it
- 29D3
- Campiello Querini Stampalia, Castello
- 041 271 1411
- Tue–Thu, Sun 10–6; Fri, Sat 10–10
- San Zaccaria
- Moderate

**MUSEO STORICO NAVALE** ✪✪

The Naval Museum records the illustrious maritime past of Venice with a magnificent collection of ship models, pictures and relics housed in an old granary near the Arsenale (► 33), which was the naval base of the Republic. The exhibits range from models of the galleys that fought the corsairs and Turks to the human torpedoes used in World War II. There is a special section devoted to the gondola and other Venetian craft, with actual boats displayed in part of the Arsenale itself.

- 29F2
- Campo San Biagio, Castello
- 041 520 0276
- Mon–Fri 8.45–1.30, Sat 8.45–1
- Arsenale
- Inexpensive

**PALAZZO CONTARINI DE BOVOLO** ✪

The Palazzo Contarini de Bovolo can unfortunately only be seen from the outside. It does, however, have a remarkable spiral staircase in its open courtyard on the Calle della Vida, close to the Campo Manin. The Bovolo Staircase (appropriately, *bovolo* means snail shell in Venetian dialect) is a remarkably delicate feat of architecture and is best seen by moonlight.

- 28C3
- Calle dei Risi, San Marco
- 041 270 2464
- Apr–end Oct daily 10–6; Nov–end Mar Sat–Sun 10–4
- Rialto
- Moderate

## PALAZZO DARIO ✪

28C2
Calle Barbaro
Not open to public
Giglio

This must surely have the most picturesque façade of any Venetian palace, made even more interesting by the fact it leans alarmingly. It was built in the 1480s and was probably the work of architect Pietro Lombardo. The use of the beautiful inlaid coloured marbles is also seen in his masterpiece, Santa Maria dei Miracoli (▶ 62). There has been a long-standing legend that the Palazzo Dario is cursed. To get the best view look over from the Santa Maria del Giglio landing stage or when taking a trip on the Grand Canal.

Below: *Ceiling detail in the Palazzo Mocenigo*

## PALAZZO DUCALE (▶ 20, TOP TEN)

## PALAZZO GRASSI ✪

28B2
Campo San Geremia
Closed at time of writing; enquire at tourist office
Guglie

This palace on the Grand Canal is a classic vast 18th-century palace with notable frescoes but was much modernized in the 1980s when it was acquired by the Fiat car company and used as an exhibition space. It was bought by the Venice authorities in 2004 and was subsequently sold to French billionaire François Pinault, who is to house his suberb art collection in the palazzo.

## PALAZZO LABIA 

28B4
Campo San Geremia
041 524 2812
By appointment Wed, Thu, Fri 3–4 (phone to arrange viewing on morning of visit)
Guglie
Phone to inquire

The Palazzo Labia, on the Campo San Geremia and the Fondamenta San Giobbe (not far from the Santa Lucia rail station), is now the headquarters of the Italian broadcasting service, RAI. It contains one of the loveliest rooms in Venice, decorated by the elder Tiepolo with gloriously coloured frescoes of Antony and Cleopatra in 16th-century dress and dramatic perspectives.

## PALAZZO MOCENIGO 

28B3
Salizzada San Stae, Santa Croce
041 721 798
Apr–end Oct Tue–Sun 10–5; Nov–end Mar Tue–Sun 10–4
San Stae
Moderate

This was the home of one of the oldest and grandest Venetian families until recent years. The nine elegantly furnished rooms of the 17th-century palazzo provide a rare insight into 18th-century Venetian noble life. Richly gilded and painted, these rooms, with their fine furniture and Murano glass chandeliers, still have a private feeling about them. Many of the paintings, friezes and frescoes are by Jacopo Guarana. The building also houses a library and a collection of period costume, together with a small exhibition of antique Venetian textiles.

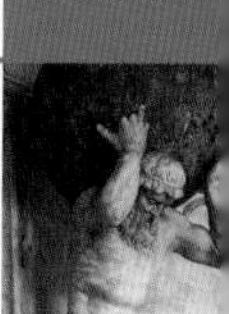

### PIAZZA SAN MARCO (➤ 21, TOP TEN)

### PIETÀ 

This has been used for concerts since the 17th century, and during the 18th century Vivaldi composed music for the choir. Music is still played here regularly on Monday evenings, when audiences can admire the oval painting by Giambattista Tiepolo on the ceiling, *The Coronation of the Virgin*. The church is only opened for concerts.

29E2
Riva degli Schiavoni, Castello
041 523 1096
Varies for concerts
San Zaccaria
Varies for concerts

### PONTE DELL'ACCADEMIA 

This is the widest crossing of the Grand Canal and surely the bridge with the loveliest of views. The canal's gentle curves, the boats and gondolas sail beneath you and the view of the dome of the Salute (➤ 24) is magical.

28B2
Canal Grande
Accademia
Canal Grande (➤ 18)

### PONTE DI RIALTO 

Built of Istrian stone in the late 16th century this was, until 1854, the only crossing of the Grand Canal and replaced a wooden bridge. A single span, decorated with relief carvings and balustrades, it is famous for its parallel rows of shops facing one another to either side of the central path. These sell mostly jewellery, leather goods, silk and shoes. The bridge commands fine views of the canal, particularly in the direction of San Marco.

29D3
Canal Grande
Rialto
Canal Grande (➤ 18)

*Close up of the Rialto Bridge, illuminated at night*

# The Canale Grande

**Distance**
Nearly 4km (2.5 miles)

**Time**
About 40 mins by *vaporetto* (public waterbus)—No 1 stops at every stop, No 82 stops at only six. You can rent a water taxi (which will be quicker) or a gondola (which will be much slower and very expensive), or take one of the organized tours from the Riva degli Schiavoni near Piazza San Marco.

**Start point**
Vallareso (San Marco) vaparetto stop

**End point**
Ferrovia vaparetto stop

**Lunch**
After your trip wander over the Ponte degli Scalzi into the Santa Croce district, an area where you will find better value for money than on the main tourist track.

Venice's main thoroughfare is the Grand Canal which—instead of taxis, buses and cars—is thronged with gondolas, waterbuses and motor launches. Its sides are lined with aristocratic *palazzi*, ranging in condition from crisply restored and maintained to melancholy, crumbling and neglected.

*Leaving from San Marco Vallareso, pass Harry's Bar on the right (➤ 96) and the imposing 17th-century customs house (➤ 37) on the left. You will see the baroque church of Santa Maria della Salute also to the left (➤ 24) followed by the marble façade of the Palazzo Dario built in 1487 (➤ 46). Next on the left is the oddly squat building, the Palazzo Venier dei Leioni, now home to the Collezione Peggy Gugenheim (➤ 37). Shortly before the Accademia footbridge, constructed in 1932, is the Palazzo Barbaro on the right where Monet, Whistler and Henry James all stayed. Beyond the bridge, on the left, is the Gallerie dell'Accademia (➤ 19).*

*Water taxi moored in front of the Ponte dei Scalzi on the Grand Canal*

After the Accademia bridge are two palazzi on the left, Palazzo Querini, home to the British Consulate, and Palazzo Loredan dell'Ambasciatore with its fine Gothic façade. Just beyond the next waterbus stop, on the right, is Browning's former home, Ca' Rezzonico (► 35), now a museum of 18th-century Venice. Look to either side for more striking palazzi, including the massive Palazzo Guistinian on the left, where Wagner composed the second act of *Tristan and Isolde* in 1858. Crowds get off at the next stop, San Tomà, giving you the chance to look across to see Palazzo Mocenigo (► 46), where Byron lived with his unruly mistress, Margherita Cogni and a menagerie of pets including a monkey, a fox and a wolf. The next bridge, the famous Rialto (► 47), is lined with shops. Round the corner is the Pescheria on the left and the striking Ca' d'Oro (► 33) on the right.

*Farther on, all on the left, are baroque Ca' Pesaro (► 34), the baroque church of San Stae (► 58) and the magnificent Renaissance Palazzo Vendramin Calergi, where Wagner died in 1883. The boat stops at San Marcuola, and you can see the church with its unfinsihed brick façade. Across the water are the 17th-century Fondaco dei Turchi (Turkish) warehouses. The final bridge is Ponte dei Scalzi.*

## PUNTALAGUNA 

www.salve.it
28C2
Campo Santo Stefano, San Marco
041 529 3582
Mon–Fri 2.30–5.30
Accademia
Free

This state-of-the-art, multimedia information centre run by Venice's water authority gives information about the canal system and the lagoon, and the work going on to safeguard the future of the city and its buildings.

## IL REDENTORE 

28C1
Campo Redentore, Giudecca Island
041 523 1415
Mon–Sat 10–5, Sun 1–5; closed Sun in Jul & Aug
Redentore
Inexpensive

This is best seen across the water from the centre of Venice. Indeed, its architect, Palladio, who was commissioned to design it as an act of thanksgiving for the ending of a 16th-century plague, intended it to catch and hold the distant eye. The façade and the interior together form a magnificent example of what came to be known as Palladian architecture. On the third Sunday of July, a bridge of boats is constructed across the Giudecca Canal for the celebration of the Feast of the Redeemer (Redentore). The church is dramatically floodlit at night.

## RIVA DEGLI SCHIAVONI 

29E2
San Zaccaria

The Riva degli Shiavoni, or 'The Waterfront of the Slavs', is the principal waterside promenade of Venice, running eastwards from the Doges' Palace to the Ca' di Dio canal, where its name changes and then continuing to the Giardini (public gardens). After the Doges' Palace and the adjoining State Prison comes the Hotel Danieli (► 101) and a succession of other grand hotels facing the Basin of San Marco. The wide, paved Riva, broken by a succession of bridges over canals, is cluttered with café tables and souvenir-sellers' stalls at its western end, while its waterside is busy with vaporetto piers and the pleasure boats and tugs that moor there. Leading from the Riva to the north are many alleys and archways running into the maze of the city and to a few squares, notably the Campo San Zaccaria and the Campo Bandera e Moro.

## SAN CASSIANO ✪

This sumptuous church, with its pillars draped in crimson and an attractive 13th-century campanile, is worth visiting for Tintoretto's majestic *Crucifixion* (1565–1568). The other two paintings by the artist have been heavily restored.

- 28C3
- Campo San Cassiano, San Polo
- 041 721 408
- Apr–end Sep daily 10–12, 5.30–7; Oct–end Mar daily 10–12, 4.30–6
- San Stae/Rialto
- Free

Opposite above: *Il Redentore seen from Zattere across the water*
Left: *Interior of San Giacomo dell'Orio*

## SAN FRANCESCO DELLA VIGNA ✪

This is a large church in the less-visited northeast of the city near the Arsenale, and its huge campanile is sometimes mistaken for that of San Marco from a distance. It contains beautiful paintings—although none of the first rank—including a delightful 15th-century *Madonna and Child Enthroned* by Antonio da Negroponte.

- 29E3
- Campo di San Francesco, Castello
- 041 520 6102
- Daily 8–12.30, 3–7
- Ospedale/Celestia
- Free

## SAN GEREMIA E LUCIA ✪

Standing on the corner of the Grand Canal and the Canale di Cannaregio, this vast, light, plain church is now remarkable for housing the body of Santa Lucia, which was removed from her own church when it was demolished to make way for the rail station that was to be named after her. Wearing a gold mask and a red and gold robe, she lies in a glass case.

- 28B4
- Campo San Geremia, Cannaregio
- Mon–Fri 8.30–12, 3.30–6.30, Sun 9.30–12, 5.30–6.30
- San Marcuola/Ferrovia
- Free

## SAN GIACOMO DELL'ORIO ✪✪

A busy parish church in a quiet campo in the west of the city, where the only visitors are likely to be those walking to the Piazzale Roma to catch a bus. Its styles of architecture and decoration reflect the growth of Venice: pillars from Byzantium and one of the two 'ship's keel' roofs (like an inverted wooden ship) in Venice—the other is in Santo Stefano (► 64); paintings by Venetian masters, including Veronese; and, in comic contrast, a funny little relief carving of a knight—almost a cartoon character—on the outside wall.

- 28B4
- Campo San Giacomo dell'Orio, Santa Croce
- 041 524 0672
- Mon–Sat 10–5, Sun 1–5
- San Stae/ Riva di Biasio
- Inexpensive

28C3
Campo San Giacomo, San Polo
Mon–Sat 7–12, 3–6
Rialto
Free

## SAN GIACOMO DI RIALTO

Standing among the fruit and vegetable market stalls at the foot of the Rialto Bridge, this the oldest church in the city—said to have been founded in the early 5th century. It has grown many architectural and decorative curiosities, including a rare brick dome; over-large baroque altarpieces; and a large, 15th-century 24-hour clock on the façade. The church faces the market square, which was once used by Venetian bankers, money changers and insurance brokers—including, presumably, Shakespeare's Shylock.

28A5
Campo San Giobbe, Cannaregio
041 524 1889
Call for hours
Ponte dei Tre Archi
Good Inexpensive

## SAN GIOBBE

Another remote church to the northwest of the city that is often locked. Dedicated to the Old Testament figure Job, it is worth a visit to see those of its paintings that have not been removed to the Gallerie dell'Accademia, including a triptych by Antonio Vivarini. Currently being restored.

29E3
Fondamenta dei Greci, Castello
041 522 6581
Daily 9–5
San Zaccaria
Inexpensive

## SAN GIORGIO DEI GRECI

The church is quickly recognizable by its dangerously tilted 16th-century campanile, caused by gradual subsidence. The church of the Greek community, many of whom were refugees from Constantinople when it was taken by the Turks in the 15th century, has strong Byzantine and Greek Orthodox decoration.

## SAN GIORGIO MAGGIORE (▶ 22, TOP TEN)

29E2
Campo Bandiera e Moro, Castello
041 520 5906
Mon–Sat 9–11, 3.30–5.30
Arsenale Free

## SAN GIOVANNI IN BRAGORA

This fascinating little parish church, where Antonio Vivaldi was baptized, lies hidden in a quiet campo off the Riva degli Schiavoni, and a plaque outside records the date of the baptism as 6th May 1678. Among the paintings in the church is a lovely, peaceful *Madonna and Child with Saints* by Bartolomeo Vivarini. Over the high altar there is another highlight, the painting of the *Baptism of Christ* (1492) by Cima da Conegliano.

*Golden interior of San Giovanni in Bragora*

*St. Jerome and fellow saints by Giovanni Bellini in the church of San Giovanni Crisostomo*

**SAN GIOVANNI CRISOSTOMO**

Just a few minutes' walk north from the Rialto is San Giovanni Crisostomo, or St. John the Golden-Tongued, a small, busy, Venetian parish church and an excellent example of Renaissance architecture. Patronized by the Archbishop of Constantinople, its architect, Mauro Codussi, based his design around the Greek cross form. Richly decorated, it is remarkable for a lovely painting of saints, *SS. Jerome, Christopher and Louis of Toulouse* by Giovanni Bellini.

29D3
Campo San Giovanni Crisostomo, Cannaregio
041 520 5906
Mon–Sat 8.30–12, 3.30–5, Sun 3.30–5.30
Rialto
Free

**SAN MARTINO** 

This is a lovely, little-visited church near the Arsenale, and it is probable that the wooden angels and cherubs around the organ were carved by craftsmen who decorated the great galleys in the dockyard. It has another spectacular ceiling painted with an *Ascension into Heaven*, past the pillars of an atrium, that seems to grow out of the architecture. The profusion of monuments and paintings makes this a very Venetian church, and outside in the wall is one of the now-rare 'lion's mask' letter boxes (mailboxes) for notes that decounce enemies of the state.

29E3
Campo San Martino, Castello
Daily 8–11, 4.30–7
Arsenale
Free

28C2
Campo San Maurizio, San Marco
041 241 1840
Daily 9.30–8.30
Giglio
Free

## SAN MAURIZIO

This faces the square on the well-trodden route between San Marco and the Accademia Bridge, where antiques markets are occasionally held. Rebuilt in 1806, it is a handsome, plain church in neoclassical style. In 2004 it opened as a Vilvadi exhibition centre. The cool and elegant interior now displays a series of exhibits of the life and times of the Venetian composer, with old musical instruments taking a prominent position. You can buy all manner of CDs, tapes and DVDs relating to the composer and you can reserve concert tickets for events at Pietà (► 47).

*Detail of an angel in the church of San Moisè*

28C2
Campo San Moisè, San Marco
041 528 5840
Mon–Sat 9.30–12.30
Vallaresso (San Marco)
Free

## SAN MOISÈ

The over-elaborate baroque façade of San Moisè, described as the clumsiest church in Venice, commands the attention of those walking towards San Marco from the Accademia Bridge. Its interior is just as odd: The high altar appears at first sight to be a bizarre rock garden but turns out to be a tableau of *Moses on Mount Sinai Receiving the Tablets*. The building is in startling contrast to the smooth Hotel Bauer Grünwald (► 100) next door.

28A2
Campo San Nicolò, Dorsoduro
041 275 0382
Mon–Sat 10–12, 4–6, Sun 4–6
San Basili/Ca' Rezzonicao
Free

## SAN NICOLÒ DEI MENDICOLI

This ornate yet modest parish church in a poor district of the city near the docks is one of Venice's oldest churches. Restored by British contributions to the Venice in Peril Fund in 1977, its gilded wooden statues gleam anew. Built between the 12th and 15th centuries and well-stocked with statuary and paintings, it is a good goal when exploring the hinterland of the western end of the Zattere and visiting the nearby churches of San Sebastiano and Angelo Raffaele.

### SAN NICOLÒ DA TOLENTINI ✪

This colossal church with a vast, pillared Corinthian portico is close to the Piazzale Roma and is popular for weddings Embedded in the exterior (under the porch) you can see a cannon ball, left by the Austrians during the siege of 1849. Inside, it is elaborate, enriched with sculpture and paintings.

- 28B3
- Campo dei Tolentini, Santa Croce
- 041 522 2160
- Daily 9–12, 4–6
- Piazzale Roma
- Free

### SAN PANTALÒN ✪✪✪

This typically Venetian baroque church probably makes a more immediate impact on the visitor than any church in Venice. On entering and looking up, the vast flat ceiling is painted with one enormous view of a mass ascent into Heaven. This startling scene also includes the life and martyrdom of San Pantalòn and was painted at the end of the 17th century and the beginning of the 18th. A typically quirky Venetian postscript is the fate of the artist, Gian Antonio Fumiani, who, as he completed his work, stepped back to admire it better, fell from the scaffolding to his death and was buried in the church he had decorated so memorably. The church also contains smaller works by Veronese and Vivarini. Like several other Venetian churches, it has no façade as its builders ran out of money.

- 28B3
- Campo San Pantalòn, Dorsoduro
- 041 523 5893
- Sun–Fri 3.30–7, 4.30–7
- San Tomà
- Free

### SAN PIETRO DI CASTELLO ✪

As it stands forlornly on its little island at the far eastern extremity of Venice, the church seems to be dreaming of past glories. This was the first of the central Venetian islands to be settled, and the church became the cathedral of Venice in AD775, remaining so until 1807, when the Basilica di San Marco, formerly the Doges' private chapel, took its place. Its isolation here throughout the life of the Venetian Republic was a deliberate attempt to minimize the influence of the Pope and Rome. It overlooks a usually deserted stretch of grass and trees. Inside, the church, which was built to a Palladian design in the 16th century, is lofty and rather grand but, above all, neglected.

- Off map 29F3
- Campo San Pietro, Isola di San Pietro
- 041 523 8950
- Mon–Sat 9–6, Sun 1–6
- Giardini
- Inexpensive

Above: *The colossal church of San Nicolò da Tolentini*

# A Stroll from San Marco

**Distance**
2km (1.25 miles)

**Time**
1 hour plus stops

**Start point**
Piazza San Marco
29D2

**End point**
Ponte di Rialto
29D3

**Lunch**
Campo Santo Stefano (➤ 37) is a charming, quiet and unspoilt square with several restaurants and cafés, including Paolin (➤ 98), one of the best places for ice cream in the city.

Start in Piazza San Marco (➤ 21) taking in all the sights.

*Facing the Basilica take the right-hand corner past the Campanile and the Palazzo Ducale to the waterfront and turn right. Continue along the canal to Calle Vallaresso. Continue to the T-junction and turn left and into Campo San Moise with the elaborate church of San Moise (➤ 54). Cross the bridge into Calle Larga 22 Marzo, then bear left at the end and on into Campo Santa Maria del Giglio (➤ 62). Leave the church on your right and bearing right, cross the two bridges into Campo San Maurizio, passing the church of the same name (➤ 54). Continue over the next bridge to Campo Santo Stefano (➤ 37).*

This square is one of the lovliest in Venice and a great place for lunch or just for people watching.

*Pass the church of Santo Stefano (➤ 64) on your right and over the bridge into Campo Sant'Angelo. Follow the canal immediately right to Calle Caotorta, cross the bridge, turn left and follow along the side of the newly restored Teatro la Fenice (➤ 68) out into Campo San Fantin.*

Campo San Fantin is a meeting place for theatregoers, and the stunning Fenice hosts superb concerts and operas.

*In the left-hand corner of the square take Calle della Verona and continue along, turning right into Calle della Mandola at the end. Proceed over the canal into Campo Manin. Cross the square, taking the left-hand corner into Salizzada San Luca and into the next square, keeping left into Calle San Lucca, which takes you into Calle Fabbri, one of the city's major shopping streets. Turn left and then first right. Keep straight on past the church of San Salvador (➤ 57) into Marzarieta Due Aprile. Continue on to San Bartolomeo and turn left to the Rialto Bridge (➤ 47).*

### SAN POLO

The church stands in the largest square in the city after San Marco. It's works of art include fine bronze statues of saints on the high altar and notable paintings by Tintoretto and both Tiepolos, including 18 paintings of *The Stations of the Cross* by the younger Tiepolo.

28C3
Campo San Polo, San Polo
041 275 0462
Mon–Sat 9–6, Sun 1–6
San Silvestro/San Tòma
Inexpensive

### SAN SALVADOR

This is regarded as one of the finest and most beautiful Renaissance churches in Italy and a change from so many Byzantine and Gothic buildings seen in Venice. Principally admired for its internal architecture, its works of art feature two paintings by Titian. *The Annunciation* is found at the end of the right-hand aisle and if you are in any doubt as to the artist, look for the autograph 'Tizianus, fecit, fecit'. The other, *The Transfiguration*, hangs over the high altar.

29D3
Campo San Salvador, San Marco
041 523 6717
Mon–Sat 9–12, 4–6.30, Sun 4–6.30
Rialto
Free

*San Salvador*

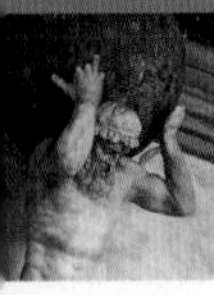

Right: *The sumptious interior of San Sebastiano*
Opposite: *The campanile and façade of the church of San Trovaso*

## SAN SEBASTIANO ✪✪✪

28A2
Campo San Sebastiano, Dorsoduro
041 270 0462
Mon–Sat 9–6, Sun 1–6
San Basilio/Ca' Rezzonico
Inexpensive

The most important of the three major churches near the docks, it belongs to the great painter Paolo Veronese, who decorated it and is buried there. His works are everywhere in the church, including the open doors of the organ and the ceiling, in the chancel, the sacristy and the gallery, where he painted frescoes on the walls. In all, he painted here the richest and most comprehensive exhibition of his own work and one that no admirer of Venetian art should miss. The interior of the church was restored during the 1980s and 1990s. It's worth using the audioguide.

## SAN STAE ✪✪

28C4
Campo San Stae, Canal Grande, Santa Croce
041 275 0462
Mon–Sat 10–5, Sun 1–5
San Stae
Inexpensive

Despite its handsome interior, this church is at its best viewed from the outside. Its neoclassical façade, decorated with joyous baroque statuary, provides one of the most striking views on the Grand Canal. Inside the finest paintings are Tiepolo's *Martyrdom of St. Bartholomew* and Piazetta's *Martyrdom of St. James the Great.* The church is used for art exhibitions and concerts.

## SAN TROVASO ✪

This is a huge Palladian church with two identical façades because, it is said, two rival 16th-century families each wanted to be the first to enter and so could do so simultaneously. The interior is lofty, light and peaceful; outside, the campo in front of the two main doors is a pleasant place to sit in the sun away from the city bustle.

- 28B2
- Campo San Trovaso, Dorsoduro
- 041 522 2133
- Accademia/Zattere
- Mon–Fri 8–11, 3–6, Sat 8–11, 3–7, Sun 8.30–1
- Free

## SAN ZACCARIA ✪✪✪

The massive 16th-century church—with traces of its predecessors—is filled with paintings. The most celebrated of these is Bellini's *Madonna and Four Saints* (1505) in the second chapel on the left. During the Venetian Republic, the nunnery attached to the church was favoured by rich families as a refuge for their unattached daughters. There is also a permanently waterlogged crypt where eight early Doges are interred.

- 29E2
- Campo San Zaccaria, Castello
- 041 522 1257
- Mon–Sat 10–12, 4–6, Sun 11–12, 4–6
- San Zaccaria
- Free; inexpensive to chapels, sacristry and crypt

## SANT'ALVISE ✪

Although one of the most remote churches in the city, this is a useful destination for a long walk including the Madonna dell'Orto (► 43) and the Ghetto (► 39). Its most notable painting (by Tiepolo) having been removed to the Gallerie dell'Accademia, the church's principal feature is now a spectacular but rather clumsily executed painted trompe l'oeil ceiling, depicting Heaven as seen from a grandiose courtyard. This is a somewhat cruder version of the extraordinary painted ceiling in San Pantalòn (► 55).

- 28C5
- Campo Sant'Alvise, Canneregio
- 041 524 4664
- Mon–Sat 10–5, Sun 1–5
- Sant'Alvise
- Inexpensive

## SANTA MARIA ASSUNTA (GESUITI) ✪✪

29D4
Campo dei Gesuiti, Cannaregio
041 528 6579
Daily 10–12, 3–6
Fondamenta Nuove
Free

The early 18th-century Jesuits built their church to impress, and the statuary along the skyline of its pediment gives a hint of what is within. Inside, the pillars and floor seem to be hung with green and white damask silk, which is also draped and ruffled around the pulpit on the north wall, but it all turns out to be marble.

## SANTA MARIA DEL CARMELO (CARMINI) ✪

28A2
Campo Carmini, Dorsoduro
041 522 6553
Mon–Sat 7.30–12, 3–7, Sun 4.30–7.30
San Basilio/Ca' Rezzonico
Free

Near the Campo Santa Margherita, this is a large and sombre 14th-century church, displaying many fine paintings, including a series in the nave illustrating the history of the Carmelite Order.

## SANTA MARIA DELLA FAVA 

29D3
Campo Rubbi, San Marco
041 522 4601
Mon–Sat 8.30–12, 4.30–6.30, Sun 8.30–12
Rialto
Free

On a back route from San Marco to the Rialto, the church of Santa Maria della Fava translates as 'St. Mary of the Bean' after a popular cake called *fave dolce* (sweet beans) once produced by a nearby bakery and traditionally eaten on All Souls' Day (1 November). The church is also known as Santa Maria della Consolazione. It is a high-ceilinged 18th-century church decorated in grey statuary by Bernardi, the teacher of Canova, and has a lovely early painting by Tiepolo, *The Education of the Virgin.* A sombre contrast is the *Madonna and Child with St. Philip Neri* by Giambattista Piazetta.

## SANTA MARIA FORMOSA ✪

29D3
Campo Santa Maria Formosa, Castello
041 523 4645
Mon–Sat 10–5, Sun 1–5
San Zaccaria
Inexpensive

The 15th-century church dominates a large square enlivened by cafés and market stalls. Designed by Mauro Codussi in 1492, it was revamped according to Renaissance ideals while retaining its original Byzantine plan. The dome was destroyed by a bomb in 1916 but was rebuilt in 1921. The church is filled with interesting monuments and paintings, including works by Vivarini *(The Madonna of Mercy),* and Palma il Vecchio *(The Martyrdom of St. Barbara).* Outside, at the base of the campanile, is the carved stone mask of a bearded man 'leering in brutal degradation', as described by John Ruskin, who could hardly bring himself to look at it.

Above: *Santa Maria del Carmelo viewed from across the canal*
Opposite: *Fine art inside Santa Maria Formosa*

28C2
Campo Santa Maria del Giglio, San Marco
041 275 0462
Mon–Sat 10–5, Sun 1–5
Giglio
Inexpensive

**SANTA MARIA DEL GIGLIO**

This appears the most worldly church in Venice because the carvings on its façade depict fortified cities and warships. These commemorate the naval and diplomatic career of Antonio Barbaro, whose family paid for the building of the façade as his monument. The interior contains paintings by Tintoretto.

**SANTA MARIA GLORIOSA DEI FRARI** **(➤ 23, TOP TEN)**

29D3
Campo dei Miracoli, Cannaregio
041 275 0462
Mon–Sat 9–6, Sun 1–6
Ca d'Oro/Rialto
Inexpensive

**SANTA MARIA DEI MIRACOLI** 

One of the most exquisite small buildings in Venice, this church has often been described as looking like a jewel box. Built in the 15th century of softly coloured marble, it stands beside a canal with such elegance that its design needs no embellishment to satisfy the eye. When closed, the outer doors are often left open so that the interior, which is as lovely as the exterior, can be admired through an inner glass door.

Have a good look around the outside before venturing in. The church was built to house an image of the Virgin painted in 1409 by Nicolò di Pietro, which had been placed in a street shrine. Becoming exceedingly popular, and credited with miraculous powers, Pietro Lombardo was commissioned to build the church, a Renaissance triumph.

Inside the marble theme continues in brilliant tones, with some of the most wonderfully intricate carving to be found in any church in the city. Lombardo and his sons, Tullio and Antonio, executed an array of beautifully sculpted saints leading to the raised choir. Look up to admire the striking celing, covered with 50 *Saints and Prophets* (1528) by Pier Pennacchi. The church is understandably a popular wedding venue.

*White and blue detail on the church of Santa Maria dei Miracoli*

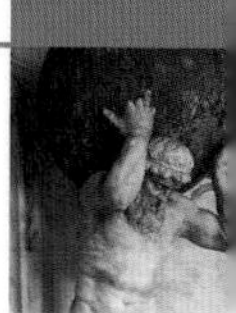

## SANTA MARIA DI NAZARETH (SCALZI) ✪✪

Close to the rail station, the church is well placed for those wanting a first, or last, look at something intensely Venetian. The *scalzi* were 'barefooted' Carmelite friars who came here in the mid-17th century and commissioned the church. The ornate baroque façade is an indication of the sumptuous but gloomy interior of multi-coloured marble, statuary and 18th-century paintings. Appropriately, the last of the doges, Ludovico Manin, is buried there.

- 28B4
- Fondamenta Scalzi, Cannaregio
- 041 715 115
- Daily 7–11.50, 4–6.50
- Ferrovia
- Free

*Huge marbled pillars adorn the church of the Scalzi*

## SANTA MARIA DELLA SALUTE (➤ 24, TOP TEN)

## SANTI APOSTOLI ✪

Located at the eastern end of the Strada Nuova, there has been a church on this site since the 9th century, and the present 16th-century church incorporates some parts of the early building, with the interior reflecting some 18th-century additions. The church is worth visiting just for *The Communion of Santa Lucia* by the elder Tiepolo in the delightful 15th-century Corner family chapel. The exceptionally tall 17th-century campanile, crowned by an onion dome (which was added 50 years later), is a well-known Venetian landmark.

- 29D4
- Campo dei Santi Apostoli, Cannaregio
- 041 523 8297
- Mon–Sat 7.30–11.30, 5–7, Sun 8.30–12, 4.15–6.30
- Ca' d'Oro
- Free

## SANTI GIOVANNI E PAOLO (➤ 25, TOP TEN)

*The richly decorated church of Santo Stefano*

28C2x
Campo Francesco Morosini, San Marco
041 522 5061
Mon–Sat 10–5, Sun 1–5
Accademia/San Samuele
Inexpensive

## SANTO STEFANO

This large, handsome church has one of only two 'ship's keel' roofs—like a huge, inverted wooden hull—in the city (the other is in San Giacomo dell'Orio). Richly painted and decorated with inlaid, multi-coloured marble, the high Gothic interior is one of the city's loveliest. It is the only church in Venice to be built directly over a canal. The church contains paintings by Tintoretto, including the highly theatrical *Agony in the Garden* and *Last Supper*. Outside are cloisters and a leaning 16th-century campanile.

29E3
Calle Furlani, Castello
041 522 8828
Apr–end Oct Tue–Sat 9.30–12.30, 3.30–6.30, Sun 9.30– 12.30; Nov–end Mar Tue–Sat 10–12.30, 3–3, Sun 10–12.30
San Zaccaria/Arsenale
Moderate

## SCUOLA DI SAN GIORGIO DEGLI SCHIAVONI

This tiny, initimate building was set up in 1451 to look after the interests of Venice's Dalmatian, or Slav, population, formerly slaves but by the 15th century established as merchants and sailors. The *scuola* has the early 16th-century Vittore Carpaccio's paintings as its main attraction, an enchanting frieze illustrating the lives of three Dalmatian saints: St. George, St. Jerome and St. Tryphon. This cycle of paintings can be found on the upper part of the walls in the ground floor hall. Ranged below one of the most lavish of celings, the cycle begins with the story of *St. George Slaying the Dragon*, an exceptionally graphic and detailed painting, followed by the *Triumph of St. George, St. George Baptising the Gentiles* and the *Miracle of St. Tryphon*. The next two, the *Agony in the Garden* and the *Calling of St. Matthew,* precede three works concerning the life of St. Jerome, the best-loved being *St. Augustine in his Study* at the moment of Jerome's death—an intimate glimpse into a medieval Venetian study, complete with appealing dog.

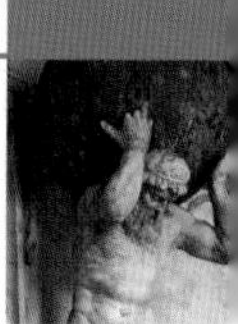

## SCUOLA GRANDE DEI CARMINI

This is the Venetian headquarters of the Carmelite order, founded in Palestine in 1235. Here the nuns undertake charitable work and attend services at the nearby church (► 60). Carmini had Giambattista Tiepolo (the elder) as its principal decorator in the 18th century and his flamboyant ceilings are the highlight of this *scoula*. His panels can be found in the Salone, on the upper floor, accessed via a sumptuous stuccoed staircase. Although the themes are, as usual, religious, his painting is sensual and so suited the mood of his time. They are not easy to understand but are based around the Carmelite emblem, the scapular, and are gloriously audacious works of art and triumph of trompe l'oeil perspective.

- 28A2
- Campo dei Carmini (near Campo Santa Margherita), Dorsoduro
- 041 528 9420
- Apr–end Oct Mon–Sat 9–6, Sun 9–4; Nov–end Mar daily 9–4,
- Ca' Rezzonico
- Moderate

## SCOULA GRANDE DI SAN GIOVANNI EVANGELISTA

One of the six Scoula Grande and not generally open to the public but it is worth a visit for its splendid exterior. Located in a tiny square near the Frari, a beautiful Renaissance complex, it was designed by Mauro Codussi in 1454 and has a stunning archway designed by Pietro Lombardo in 1481. The eagle crowning the arch is the symbol of St. John the Evangalist. The interior is remarkable for a converging double staircase that leads to the Albergo, the main conference room, hung with scenes from the life of St. John. Admission to the building is possible when exhibitions or concerts are being held or sometimes on request.

- 28B3
- Campiello de la Scoula, San Polo
- 041 718 8234 to arrange a visit
- San Tòma/Pizzale Roma
- Donation

*The entrance to the small Renaissance courtyard of the Scoula Grande di San Gionvanni Evangelista*

# Around and about in Dorsoduro

**Distance**
3.5km (2 miles)

**Time**
2 hours plus stops

**Start point**
Ponte dell'Accademia
28B2

**End point**
Santa Maria Gloriosa
28B3

**Lunch**
Campo Santa Margherita (► 36) is a lively square with a choice of restaurants and cafés.

Start on the south side of the bridge, facing the Gallerie dell'Accademia (► 19). Turn left into Rio Terra Antioni Fosca and continue to the waterfront, passing the large church of the Gesuati with ceiling and altar paintings by Tiepolo.

*Turn right at the end along the Zaterre, turning right just before the bridge. Continue along by the canal. On your left is the boatyard of Squero di San Trovaso (► 68) and the church of the same name (► 59). Take a left at the second bridge into Calle Toletta and straight on crossing another bridge into Campo San Barnaba (► 36). Take the left corner out of the square, cross the first bridge into Rio Terrà Canal and turn left into San' Aponal. Turn right into Campo San Margherita.*

This square is a pleasant place to stop for lunch or a rest.

*Return to San' Aponal and continue along, turning right by the Scoula Grande (► 65) and the church of Santa Maria del Carmelo (► 60). Continue by the canal and cross the fourth bridge past the church of San Sebastiano (► 58) on your left. Continue ahead across Campazza San Sebastiano to go behind the church of Angelo Raffaele (► 33). Cross the bridge and turn right to walk along the Fondementa for about 500m (545 yards).*

Along the canal to the left you can see the Palazzo Cicogna with its attractive Gothic windows now used as a school.

Opposite: *Carved inlaid wooden stalls of the choir in Santa Maria Gloriosa dei Frari*
Left: *Gondola repair yard at Squero di San Trovaso*
Below: *Strolling down the Fondamenta Zattere*

*The canal turns sharply left. Continue and pass one bridge. When you reach the next two bridges take the one to the right and bear left alongside the canal. Before the next two bridges turn right. Take the second bridge and turn right onto Fondamenta Minotto, leading into Calle Vinanti. As you cross the canal take the next left over the bridge with the Scoula Grande di San Rocco (➤ 26) in front of you. Turn right, keeping the scoula to the left. Ahead is the church of Santa Maria Gloriosa dei Frari (➤ 23) with its superb interior.*

29D4
San Giovanni e Paolo, Castello
Ospedale Civile

## SCOULA SAN MARCO

Another magnificent *scoula* with a fine exterior stands next to the church of Santi Giovanni e Paolo and now houses the main hospital and can be visited by appointment only. Its most interesting works of art, relief carvings incoporating startling perspectives, can be seen on the outside wall facing the campo.

## SCOULA GRANDE DI SAN ROCCO (➤ 26, TOP TEN)

28B2
On the San Trovaso Canal (near the Zattere), Dorsoduro
Zattere

## SQUERO DI SAN TROVASO

This is a picturesque boatyard where gondolas have been built and repaired for hundreds of years, and it is still full of activity. Even though it is closed to the public you can get great photographs of the upturned gondolas awaiting repair, with the church of San Trovaso as a backdrop, all from the opposite side of the canal.

**www.**teatrolafenice.org
28C2
Campo San Fantin, San Marco
041 786 611. Call centre 041 2424
Tours only; reserve in advance by person or telephone, fax or internet. Tours last 45 mins
Tours moderate
Ca' Rezzonico

## TEATRO LA FENICE

The *fenice* (phoenix) has finally risen from the ashes. The theatre was utterly destroyed by fire on 29 January 1996. More than a year later two electricians were sentenced for arson, the fire shrouded in mystery. It was not the first time the theatre had been wrecked by fire. Built by Giannantonio Silva in 1792, it had to be rebuilt after a fire in 1836. The prolonged restoration has been well worth waiting for. The new theatre—a wonderful opulent reconstruction in gilt, stucco and marble—surpasses the old. In addition the equipment and sound systems are second to none. You will need to reserve well in advance for performances but you can join a tour to see all its glory.

Left: *The gilt sign and phoenix of La Fenice has risen once again*
Above: *Scene from a performance of* La Roi Lahore *at the rebuilt Teatro la Fenice*

## TORRE DELL'OROLOGIO (CLOCK TOWER)

The tower stands above the arch leading to the Mercerie shopping street close to the Basilica di San Marco. Designed by Mauro Codussi and built at the end of the 15th century, its remarkable, brightly enamelled clock face and its digital clock are linked with automata, which attract crowds in the Piazza. The exterior stone dial shows the 24 hours in Roman numerals; the interior face shows signs of the zodiac and phases of the moon. On the summit of the tower two large bronze figures known as the Mori (Moors) strike the hour. During Ascension Week and at Epiphany, figures of the Magi emerge to either side of the clock face and bow to the statue of the Madonna above it. It has been undergoing a lengthy restoration since 1999, the opening date still undecided.

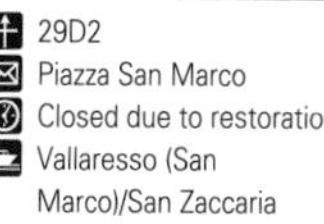

29D2
Piazza San Marco
Closed due to restoration
Vallaresso (San Marco)/San Zaccaria

*Torre dell'Orologio in Piazza San Marco*

## ZATTERE

The Zattere forms a series of f*ondamenta* (roads beside the water) along the Canal della Guidecca on the southern side of Dorsoduro. It stretches from the Stazione Máríttima in the west to the Punta della Dogna in the east, its name deriving from the unloading of heavy goods—particulary cargos of salt for the nearby warehouses—which were floated to the quayside on rafts known as *záttere.* Ventians now love to take the *passeggiata* here and it is a great place to rest, have a drink or an ice cream.

28A2–C1
Zattere, Dorsoduro
Zattere/San Basilio

# To the Gardens of Castello

**Distance**
3.5km (2 miles)

**Time**
2 hours plus stops

**Start point**
Palazzo Ducale
29D2

**End point**
Arsenale vaporetto stop
29E2

**Lunch**
Take a refreshment stop among the locals at Via Guiseppe Garibaldi.

Above: *Santa Maria della Pietà*
Opposite: *The imposing statute of Garibaldi stands in the Giardini Pubblici*

Start at the Palazzo Ducale on the edge of San Marco and turn left onto Riva degli Schiavoni. As you go over the first bridge look to the left to see the renowned Ponte dei Sospiri (Bridge of Sighs). Continuing along you can see the famous Danieli hotel—named after its first proprietor Dal Niel—before crossing the next bridge. Housed in former 15th-century palazzo it has been a hotel since the early 19th century, its interior retaining many of the original features. At this point out across the water is the Isola di San Giorgio Maggiore, with its striking church *(➤ 22).*

*Carry on along the waterfront, pausing to look back over your shoulder at the superb view. Go over the next bridge and past the church of Santa Maria della Pietà (➤ 47). Continue over two more bridges and go past the Aresenale vaporetto stop and over the next bridge into Campo San Biàgio with the Museo Storico Navale (➤ 45). Continue along Riva dei Sette Martiri as far as the Giardini Pubblici (➤ 42). After the Giardini vaporetto stop turn left into the gardens where you will see the Biennale Internazionale d'Arte in front of you. Turn left and keep bearing left until first right takes you into Viale Garibaldi with the Garibaldi monument at the end. Go through the impressive gates at the end and turn left into Via Guiseppe Garibaldi.*

This vibrant street, the widest in Venice, is in the heart of working-class Castello, where you will feel a long way from the popular narrow streets and canals of the tourist trail.

*About 150m (163 yards) on the right take the narrow alley Calle de Forno, crossing the bridge at the end. Turn left and at the canal turn right to the Arsenale (➤ 33). Cross the bridge and keep on to the church of San Martino (➤ 53). Go round the church and continue with the canal on your right until you reach Calle de Pegola. Turn down here and at the end turn right into Calle del Forni, which will take you back to the waterfront. The Arsenale vaporetto stop is almost immediately in front of you.*

# Food & Drink

Its reputation for dull, unimaginative cooking, high prices and surly service is not fair to Venice. It is true that restaurants tend to be more expensive—beware hidden costs—than those on the mainland since almost everything but some of the fish has to be imported by barge, and along the tourist trails the waiters can become as jaded as their customers, particularly in summer. That said, you can eat well in Venice.

## Origins of Venetian cuisine

Venice sits at the crossroads of the former trading routes linking Europe to the East. For centuries there was the desire for the spices of the Orient and men plying those goods would often rest up in the city leaving their influence. Exotic foods from Arabia, Turkey and Asia found their way into the local cuisine. The use of spices in the rice dishes, the addition of spiced vinegar and nuts and raisins to the sardines, and foods preserved for the sailors on the long sea journeys all contributed to a unique diet. Venetian chefs utilized the local fresh produce—vegetables, fruit, and river and sea fish—combining them with the foreign imports to produce great banquets and lavish hospitality the city was renowned for. Tastes may have simplified over the years, but the Venetian cusine still retains something of its earlier origins.

*Intimate coffee at the Café Florian—where the waiters where their badge with pride*

## Finding the real thing

Local people won't accept the mediocre food that is often on offer in a city so dominated by tourists, so you need to search out the traditional restaurants frequented by Venetians. You only have to look in the Rialto markets to see what is on offer. Two of the most familiar Venetian main dishes are acquired tastes: *fegato alla Veneziana* (sliced calves' liver with onion) and *seppie* (squid) cooked in its own black ink with *polenta* (cornmeal cake). Venetians are good at creating delectable sweets, particularly the light and creamy *tiramisú*, a delicious cold confection of chocolate, coffee, mascarpone cheese and brandy. Another way to get a taste of Italian food is to try some of the many local snacks

known as *cicheti*, usually displayed on counters and not dissimilar to Spanish tapas. These include garlicky *polpette* (meatballs), *pizzetas (*mini-pizzas), various types of seafood and slices of fried vegetables. Take a look at the selection in the windows of the old-fashioned Venetian bakeries and patisseries to see how the traditional pastries have survived. They may not always suit your palate but are worth a try. Two classic biscuits are interesting—*baicoli* and *busoli*. The first is a light, dry biscuit, its shape resembling a fish, which is best eaten with a drink or ice cream. The latter, the *busolai*, comes from the island of Burano and is seriously sweet with a hint of aniseed. For a daintier and more refined treat try some of the more sophisticated shops or cafés where you will also find the *brioscia*, the ubiquitous breakfast ingredient, the melt-in-the-mouth croissant.

Above: *Dine in style overlooking the canal*
Below: *By the water and among the flowers, diners enjoying their meal*

## Eating out

Those enjoying the higher trattoria style of cooking will not be disappointed. Venetian restaurants offer the same range of basic Italian dishes as will be found throughout the country, but their local specialties are more simple than say Florence, Bologna or Rome. For a first course try *zuppa di pesce* (fish soup), which is so full of shellfish, shrimps and white fish that it is best followed by something light, or try *prosciutto crudo* (Parma ham) with fresh figs. Fish and seafood is expensive but popular with a plentiful supply of fish coming from the Adriatic—try the *antipasto di frutti di mare*, a particular favourite. You'll find some unusual seafood too—*granseola* (spider crab), *capelonghe* (razor shells) and *schie* (miniature prawns).

## And to drink

When ordering drinks, *una ombra* (which means 'shade') will produce a glass of white house wine, unless you request *rosso* (red). Ombra comes from the old tradition of drinking wine in the shade of the piazza. Head for a *bàcaro* (a traditional wine bar), for a glass or two. A *spritz* is a popular drink in Venice (a glass of white wine served with an apertif such as Campari)—watch out, they can be strong!

Laudato mi Signore sie

# Excursions from Venice

There comes a time when even the most ardent lover of Venice needs a break from the crowds. Hop on a boat and there are plenty of other islands to explore from the busy glass-producing Murano, picturesque Burano and the natural environment of Torcello to the smaller islands dotted around the lagoon, each with its own character. Even the boat trip is an experience in itself with the refreshing breeze to clear the mind and the wonderful views back to the city. For the seaside head for the cosmopolitan Lido with its attractive early 20th-century buildings and its long sandy beach, or go farther down the coast to the busy Lido di Jésolo. Venture inland to visit the atmospheric towns of the region from romantic Verona to pretty Asolo. Take the train to Padova (Padua) or go along the coast to historic Trieste close to the Slovenian border, its busy harbour lapped by the Adriatic Sea. For a complete contrast visit the stunning Dolomite mountains, the perfect place for a summer hike or first-rate skiing in winter.

*'In the afternoon we go out on the lagoon—that is almost the most wonderful of all'*

LOGAN PEARSALL SMITH
*Letter to his mother* (1895)

*Delicate wrought-iron work on the tiny islet of San Francesco del Deserto*

# The Islands

**Scattered across nearly 500sq km (200sq miles) of the Venetian lagoon are some 40 islands. Some have a proud history of their own; some were famous for their industries; others were renowned as religious centres. Many of them acted as fortresses, gunpowder factories and stores; others were hospitals and asylums. Half of them are now deserted, while those still inhabited may be thriving communities or isolated institutions—a prison, a hospital or a religious retreat—and a few are used for public or private recreation. Some provide the fertile ground for vegetable crops to supply the Rialtos markets. Enough of them can be visited to add another dimension to a holiday in Venice. The main islands are well-serviced by vaporetto, but others can only be reached by the more expensive water taxis.**

## What to See–the islands

77B2

LN from Fondamente Nuove

Below: *Vivid reflections in Burano*

### BURANO ✪✪✪

The fishermen's and lace makers' island with a population of about 5,000 lies more than 8km (5 miles) to the northeast of Venice. While Murano (► 79) is workaday and slightly dishevelled, Burano is neat and clean and its multi-coloured cottages lining little canals make it a perfect subject for photographs. Its character has been shaped by its industries—the robust way of life of its fishermen and

boatbuilders and the delicacy of its lace makers' skills. Usually women can be seen making lace outside the doors of their cottages—although they are now dwindling in number—and their products (as well as embroidery from Hong Kong) are on sale at stalls and local shops. You can visit the **Museo del Merletto** where fine lace is beautifully displayed, and upstairs, local women ply their craft.

There are few buildings of note, but the church of San Martino contains a huge and disturbing painting of the *Crucifixion* by the elder Tiepolo and has the most alarmingly tilted campanile of them all.

**Museo del Merletto**

Piazza Galuppi 187
041 730 034
Apr–end Oct Wed–Mon 10–5, Nov–end Mar Wed–Mon 10–4
Inexpensive

**San Martino**

Piazza Galuppi
041 730 096
Daily 8–12, 3–7 Free

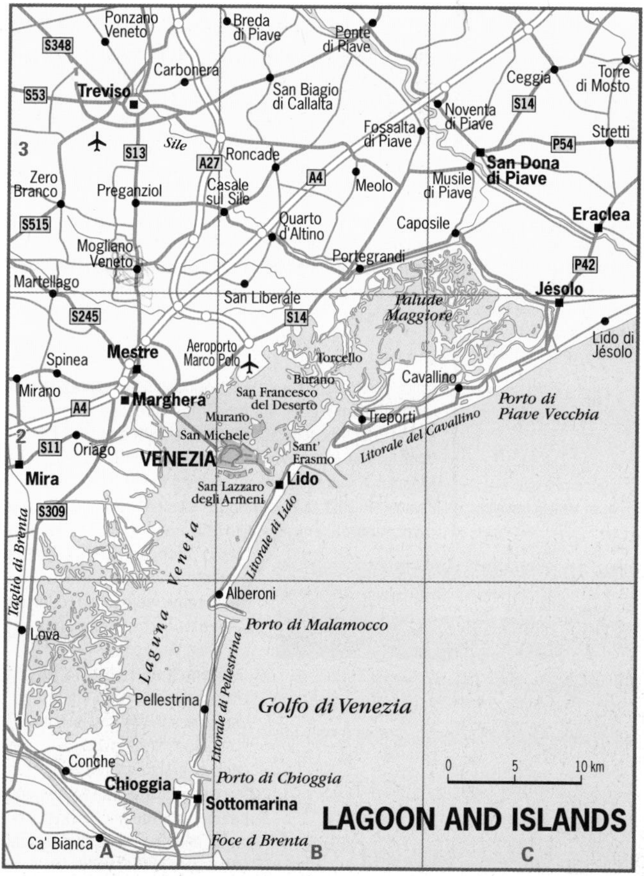

## LAGOON AND ISLANDS

77A1
Museo Civico, Fondamenta San Francesco
041 550 0911
11 from the Lido
From Piazzale Roma

## CHIOGGIA

Once an island, Chioggia is now, like Venice, connected to the mainland by a causeway; unlike Venice, several of its canals have been filled in to become roads for cars. In the far south of the lagoon, 26km (16 miles) from Venice, it has grown from a fishing port to an important town of some 55,000 inhabitants. Now, in essence, it belongs to the mainland rather than the lagoon.

Much of the town, particularly around the remaining canals, is reminiscent of Venice, and many buildings date from the 13th to 18th centuries. There are several fine churches, notably the Duomo, built between the 13th and 17th centuries, which contains a painting by the elder Tiepolo. There are a number of excellent fish restaurants near the harbour and in the Corso del Popolo.

77B2
Viale Santa Maria Elisabetta 6/a, Lido di Venezia
041 526 5721
Jun–end Sep daily 9.30–4
1 from San Zaccaria or stops on the Grand Canal
ACTV buses leave for all destinations on the Lido.

## LIDO

This is the only one of the Venetian islands to have roads, and its buses, cars and lorries are imported by ferry from the mainland. A little to the southeast of Venice, it is just over 11km (7 miles) long and 1km (0.5 miles) wide, covering the largest sand bank between the lagoon and the Adriatic. With a population of about 20,000 it is essentially a seaside holiday resort and is crowded in summer, when it is also host to the International Film Festival.

It was at its most fashionable before World War I as the architecture of its hotels and villas testifies, and its long sandy beach is still lined with wooden bathing-huts, which recall that time. Look out for some interesting art nouveau and art deco buildings. Of particular interest on the Gran Viale is the Hungaria Palace and the No. 14, the Villa Monplaisir. Another striking building is the Hotel Excelsior Palace (► 102), a neo-Moorish design, sporting its very own minaret. There's also the historic church of San Nicolò, founded in 1044, at the northern end of the island. The doge came here on Ascension Day after the ceremony of marrying Venice to the sea.

From the vaporetto bound from the Lido to San Marco, Venice is seen as it was intended it should first be seen, from the deck of a ship approaching from the sea, its towers, domes and palaces materializing between water and sky in one of the great spectacles of the world.

*View from Venice towards the Lido*

## MURANO 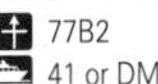

With around 5,000 inhabitants, Murano lies a short distance to the north of the city. It is an industrial island and has the feel of a small working town, although some of its factories lie derelict. Glass is its product and has been since the 13th century, when production was moved out of Venice itself because of the fire risk. Venetian glass has long been a curious mixture of the beautiful and the vulgar, whether in table-glass, ornaments, mirrors or chandeliers. Past products can be see in the **Museo Vetrario di Murano**, together with a history of glass on the island. New production can be seen in many factory showrooms to which visitors will constantly be invited.

Murano is a miniature, shabbier Venice with its own scaled-down Canal Grande, crossed by a single bridge. Its most notable building is the church of **Santa Maria e Donato**, which has a 12th-century mosaic floor and a 15th-century 'ship's keel' roof.

77B2
41 or DM

**Museo Vetratrio di Murano**
Fondamenta Giustinian 8, Isola di Murano
041 739 586
Apr–end Oct Thu–Tue 10–5; Nov–end Mar Thu–Tue 10–4
To Museo
Inexpensive

**Santa Maria e Donato**
Campo San Donato
041 739 056
Mon–Sat 9–12, 3.30–7, Sun 3.30–7
To Museo
Free

Left: *Mosaic floor in San Donato, Murano*
Below: *Glass parrots made on the island of Murano*

77B2
Daily 9:30–11.30, 3–5
Water taxi from Burano
Donation on admission

## SAN FRANCESCO DEL DESERTO

This remote and peaceful island can be reached by ferry from Burano, and the resident friars will show visitors the 13th-century cloister and the church of the hermitage, where St. Francis of Assisi is said to have stayed.

77B2
Daily one guided tour 3.25–5.15
20
Moderate

## SAN LAZZARO DEGLI ARMENI

This Armenian island can be visited to see the church, library and monastery where Lord Byron stayed in 1817 to learn Armenian.

Right: *Detail of an illuminated gospel, one of the many treasures in San Lazzaro degli Armeni*
Below: *The cemetry on the island of San Michele*

77B2
41, 42 to Cimitero (cemetry)

## SAN MICHELE

This is the cemetery island, as can be seen by its sepulchral white walls and the tall, dark cypress trees beyond. The beautiful 15th-century church of San Michele in Isola is of interest to students of Renaissance artchitecture, but the cemetery is even sadder than could be expected, for dead Venetians cannot rest there long. While the famous—such as the composer Stravinsky, the poet Ezra Pound and the ballet impresario Diaghilev—are allowed to remain, nearly all Venetians buried here are disinterred after a period and their bones scattered on a reef made of their ancestors' remains in a remote reach of the lagoon. The visitor cannot fail to be confronted by evidence that here death, as well as life, is transitory.

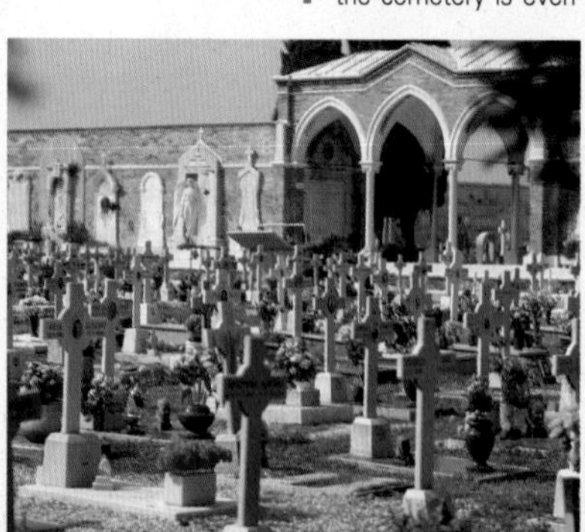

**TORCELLO** ✪✪✪

If you only visit one island make it Torcello. It was the first island to be settled by refugees from the barbarian invasion of the 5th century. At the height of its power, the population was said to have numbered 20,000, but the growth of the more distant and secure Venice, the silting of its creek and the prevalence of malaria reduced it to the level of the other small islands of the lagoon by the 15th century. Now the permanent popluation is only around 20, increased only slighty in the summer by restaurant staff.

Lying close to the mainland marshes and more than 10 km (6 miles) to the northeast of Venice, the little green island offers peace after the bustling city and relaxation in walks along its narrow footpaths. Its great monument is the cathedral of **Santa Maria dell'Assunta**, where the extraordinary Byzantine mosaics—notably a tall and compelling Madonna and Child and a vast depiction of Judgement Day—have been restored. The basilica dates from 638 and is the oldest building in Venice. It remains virtually untouched since alterations in the 11th century.

The whole island, including the cathedral, the small church of Santa Fosco, the archaeological museum, **Museo dell'Estuario** and the surrounding farmland, is easily explored and can be combined with lunch on a day-trip from Venice without making an early start or expecting a late return.

77B2
LN from Fondamente Nuove

**Basilica di Santa Maria dell'Assunta**

Torcello
041 270 2464
Mar–end Oct daily 10.30–6; Nov–end Feb daily 10–5
Moderate

**Museo dell'Estuario**

Torcello
041 270 2464
Mar–end Oct Tue–Sun 10.30–6; Nov–end Feb Tue–Sun 10–5
Moderate

*View from the bell tower over the island of Torcello*

# Isole Venezia

**Distance**
20km (12 miles)

**Time**
Allow about 2.5–3 hours without stops; up to a day with stops

**Start/end point**
San Zaccaria vaparetto stop

**Lunch**
Locanda Cipriani (€€€)
✉ Piazza Santa Fosca 29, Torcello
☎ 041 730 150
Closed Tue and Nov–end Mar

In the Lagoon north of Venice is an archipelago of flat little islands. Many of these are uninhabited or privately owned, but some have been populated for centuries. Three—Murano, Burano and Torcello—each in a different way, are interesting places to visit on a day trip from Venice.

*From San Zaccaria the boat heads southeast past the island of San Giorgio Maggiore.*

The church here (1559–80), by Palladio, contains works by Tintoretto and has excellent views from its bell tower.

*The boat then chugs round the eastern peninsula of Venice before heading northwest, past the Isola di San Michele.*

The island has been used as a graveyard since the 19th century; Diaghilev, Stravinsky and Ezra Pound are among those who lie behind its protective walls.

*North of here is the island of Murano.*

The centre of Venetian glass blowing since the 13th century, Murano has numerous factories offering guided tours and the Museo Vetrario with glass pieces from the 15th century onward. This island is like a minature Venice with its own Grand Canal.

*Next comes the island of Burano.*

Once a great lace-making hub, Burano is now more remarkable for its brightly painted houses in every hue—purple, sky blue, leaf green and more—and the alarmingly leaning tower of San Martino church. Walk in the back streets to avoid the crowds and you will see that time has stood still, the washing still hangs out and the locals tend their pretty balconies and pots of bright flowers.

*Torcello, the last island, is the most historic.*

Torcello was once a thriving community of 20,000, but started to decline in the 14th century. Now all that remain are two adjoining churches set in serene rural scenery near an old canal. The 9th- to 11th-century Cathedral of Santa Maria dell'Assunta has a charmingly expressive mosaic of the Last Judgement, while the 12th-century church of Santa Fosca is surrounded on three sides by a harmonious peristyle and has a tranquil, simple interior.

Opposite: *Bright and geometric—a doorway on the island of Burano*

# What to See Around Venice–Mainland

85B2
Piazza Garibaldi 73
0423 529 046
No direct bus to Asolo. It is possible to get a train to Bassano del Grappa, then bus towards Montebelluna and a shuttle to Asolo. Car or tour easiest.

## ASOLO

The most beautiful of the hinterland towns, Asolo lies in the foothills of the Alps 64km (40 miles) from Venice. A charming town of some 6,000 inhabitants, its old houses—sometimes arcaded at street level as is the custom in hill towns—cluster around squares and narrow streets and overlook a landscape decorated with villas and cypress trees.

85B2
Largo Corona d'Italia 35
0424 524 351
From Venezia San Lucia station

## BASSANO DEL GRAPPA

In the foothills of the Alps, nearly 80km (50 miles) northwest of Venice, this town of 37,000 inhabitants was once under Venetian rule. Formerly renowned for its school of painting, it now produces colourful pottery, which is sold in Venice and throughout northern Italy.

There are some fine old buildings and a famous covered wooden bridge—the Ponte degli Coperto—that has been rebuilt several times since the early 13th century. Bassano is noted for the strong alcoholic spirit, *grappa*. The town is a good base for exploring the mountains—particularly Monte Grappa, which was an Italian stronghold during World War I—and the battlefields Ernest Hemingway described in *A Farewell to Arms*.

Farther north and into the Alps is the handsome old town of Belluno and beyond it the Dolomite mountains and the celebrated resort of Cortina, renowned for winter sports and summer walking. Austria is also just within range of a day's excursion.

85B3
Piazza dei Martiri 7
0437 940 083
From Venezia San Lucia station

## BELLUNO

This attractive town, the capital of Belluno province and 90km (56 miles) from Venice, is at the junction of the flat plains of Veneto to the south and the stunning Dolomite mountains to the north. It claimed the accolade of 'Alpine Town of the Year in 1999' but it is often overlooked by people in their rush to see the mountains. There is much more to Belluno than being the start point for a hiking weekend in summer or a skiing holiday in winter. Its architecture reflects its close proximity to Venice and merges well with the rural style of the surrounding countryside. Highlights of the town include the spectacular views from the 12th-century Porta Rugo and from the bell tower of the 16th-century duomo. Take a break in the town's finest square, Piazza del Mercato, complete with fountain and arcaded Renaissance palaces.

## LIDO DI JÉSOLO ✪

This seaside resort is along the Adriatic coast 40km (25 miles) to the east of Venice and can be reached by bus from the city. Its sandy beach is 15km (9 miles) long and offers accommodation from hotels to villas and apartments to campsites. Although there has been a settlement here since Roman times it only developed as a thriving resort after World War I and now more than 400,000 people visit every year. You can participate in all manner of activities: sailing, horse riding, go karting and, of course, swimming as well as enjoying a vibrant nightlife.

85B2
Piazza Brescia 13
☎ 042 137 0601
The easiest way to get to Jésolo is by bus and then by boat. Enquire at the tourist office

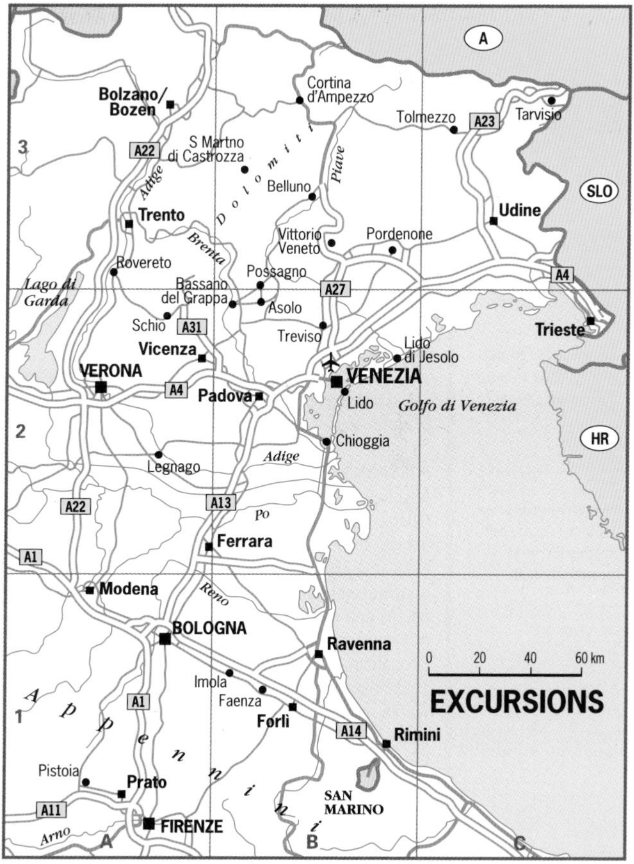

EXCURSIONS

Bolzano/Bozen
Cortina d'Ampezzo
Tolmezzo
Tarvisio
A23
A22
S Martno di Castrozza
Dolomiti
Belluno
Piave
SLO
Udine
Trento
Adige
Brenta
Vittorio Veneto
Pordenone
Rovereto
Possagno
A4
Lago di Garda
Bassano del Grappa
A27
Asolo
Schio
A31
Treviso
Trieste
Vicenza
Lido di Jesolo
VERONA
VENEZIA
A4
Padova
Lido
Golfo di Venezia
2
Chioggia
HR
Adige
Legnago
A22
A13
Po
Ferrara
A1
Modena
Reno
BOLOGNA
Ravenna
0 20 40 60 km
Imola
Faenza
A1
1
Forlì
A14
Rimini
Appennini
Pistoia
Prato
SAN MARINO
A11
FIRENZE
Arno
A
B
C
3
A

Above: *The Villa Foscari on the canalbank viewed from the Brenta Canal*

## PADOVA (PADUA) ✪✪✪

85B2
Pizzale della Stazione
0429 875 2077/;
Riviera dei Mugnai 8
0429 876 7911
From Venezia San Lucia station
53E

The nearest large town to Venice with a population of a quarter of a million, Padova can be reached by train, bus, car—or by boat. For the latter, the Burchiello and its rival the Ville del Brenta, sail between April through October from San Marco at about 9am (times and fares available from hotel concierges, travel agents and tourist information offices), cross the lagoon and cruise up the Brenta Canal, which is, in fact, a river. Stopping at several magnificent Renaissance villas on its banks and for lunch at a riverside restaurant, they arrive at Padua between 6 and 6.30pm and the 37km (23-mile) return journey to Venice is made by bus or train.

A Venetian university city since the 15th century—and rich in buildings of that century—Padova is now dominated by commerce.

## POSSAGNO 

85B3
From Venezia San Lucia station to Bassano del Grappa then bus to Possagno (1 hour)

Anyone eager to see more works of art should visit the village of Possagno, 72km (45 miles) northwest of Venice, the home of the sculptor Antonio Canova. Born here in 1757, Canova became the greatest of the neoclassical sculptors, producing smoothly graceful figures and delicate portraits, including his famous busts of Napoleon and Josephine, which are now in galleries throughout the world.

His house is now the centre of a gallery devoted to his works, mostly plaster models for statuary, and in the parish church which he gave to the village—the Tempio di Canova, inspired by the Parthenon in Athens and the Pantheon in Rome—is his tomb. However, only his body lies here; his heart remains in Venice, within the pyramid he himself designed for Titian in the great church of the Frari (► 23).

**TREVISO** ✪✪

Treviso's walled centre is full of meandering old streets and brooding canals. The medieval and Renaissance buildings of Piazza dei Signori include the church of Santa Lucia, with frescoes by Tommaso da Modena (14th century). Gothic San Nicolò contains more da Modena frescoes on the columns as well as works by Lorenzo Lotto and others, while the 15th- to 16th-century cathedral has a Titian altarpiece and an 11th-century baptistery. There is good Renaissance art in the Museo Civico.

85B2
Piazzetta Monte di Pietà
0422 547 632
From Venezia San Lucia station
8E

**TRIESTE** ✪✪

Farther east of Venice than Lido di Jésolo is the great seaport of Trieste, once part of the Austro-Hungarian Empire and now connected with Venice by rail. A little farther to the north, just across the Slovenian border, is Lipica, where the Lipizzaner white horses are bred and can be ridden.

85C2
Piazza Unita d'Italia 4B
040 347 8312
From Venezia San Lucia station
3, 6, 57, 66

*Along Treviso's Calmaggiore lined with 15th- and 16th-century houses*

85A2
Piazza Bra, Via degli Alpini 9
045 806 8680
From Venezia San Lucia station

## VERONA ✪✪✪

Verona lies west of Vicenza (► below), close to Lake Garda and some 98km (61 miles) from Venice. It is the second-biggest city in the Veneto region after Venice. It is most famous as the setting of Shakespeare's play *Romeo and Juliet* and for its Roman remains, notably a magnificent arena, which is sometimes used for performances of opera. Among Verona's other important monuments is the unusually ornate Romanesque church of San Zeno Maggiore (1123–35), with 11th–12th century bronze door panels, a 'ship's keel' ceiling (1376) and an altarpiece by Mantegna (1450s). The two main squares are the elegant Piazza dei Signori, with the 12th-century Palazzo del Comune (town hall) among its medieval and Renaissance civic gems, and the more workaday Piazza delle Erbe, with a busy market. The powerful Scaligeri family, who governed the town from 1260 to 1387, are commemorated by a 14th-century bridge leading to the Castelvecchio (with an excellent art collection) and by the Arche Scaligere, their opulent tombs.

Above: *'Wherefore art thou Romeo'—balcony scene in Verona*

85A2
Piazza Matteotti 12
0444 320 854
From Venezia San Lucia station

## VICENZA ✪✪✪

The capital of the Veneto is Vicenza, which lies 51km (32 miles) from Venice and is a handsome city, where the great architect Andrea di Palladio—a native of Padova—designed a dozen buildings.

Most famous of these is his eye-pleasingly symmetrical villa La Rotunda, which has been copied all over the world. Palladio's first public commission was the graceful double-colonnaded Basilica in Piazza dei Signori, where he also designed the Loggia del Capitaniato. Among the mass of other Palladio buildings are the Teatro Olimpico (1579), the oldest covered theatre in Europe, and many of the palazzi on Corso Andrea Palladio. The Museo Civico (in another Palladio building) has splendid Gothic and Renaissance art. Other older monuments include the Gothic churches of Santa Corona and San Lorenzo and some buildings on Contrà Porti, untouched by Palladio.

# The Dolomites

The Dolomite mountains look as if they've been carved, folded and squeezed into an extraordinary variety of gnarled crags. They are named after Frenchman Déodat Tancrè Gratet de Domomieu (1750–1801), who was responsible for discovering the chemical component that renders the local rock so different from others. Although this is Italy, the language, scenery, architecture and much of the culture has been strongly influenced by Austria, and in particular in the north of the region, on the far side of the Dolomites, nearly all the place names have versions in German.

It is possible to take tours from Venice to the mountains, where you will witness soaring peaks, deep verdant valleys, emerald lakes and enchanting mountain villages. Some tours take you as far as Cortina d'Ampezzo, one of Italy's top ski and alpine resorts. There are plenty of superb photographic opportunities. Activities in the mountains include rambling along the footpaths and picnicking, mountain biking, skiing in season and the use of chairlifts to get to see some of the most breathtaking scenery. The range of flora is extensive: Look for the gorgeous orange mountain lily, pretty saxigfrages, the purple gentian (among a dozen gentian species)—the roots of which are used to make a local liqueur—the black vanilla, globe and lady's slipper orchids, and the enigmatic devil's claw. Butterflies abound, and you may see eagles, chamois and the Alpine marmot, too.

The closest Dolomite town to Venice, lying in the foothills of the mountains, is Belluno (► 84). This is a far cry from the German-speaking northern Dolomites, but there is an Alpine air pervading. Close by is the Parco Naturale delle Dolomiti Bellunesi, an environmental project protecting the countryside and cultural heritage of the area. Tourists have been visiting since the 18th century drawn by the spectacular scenery and Alpine plants and flowers. The park is actively promoting the continuation of the traditional environment by encouraging old farming methods and thus leaving the locality virtually unchanged. This is a fascinating region and a total contrast from the low-lying area of Venice and its islands.

85B3

To Belluno from Venezia San Lucia station

By arranged tour, car or bus. Information from Venice tourist office or local travel agencies

*The Dolomites*

# Where To...



Opposite: *Campo Santa Margherita, Venice*
Above: *All dressed up for the Carnevale*

# Venice

**Prices**
Prices are for a three-course meal for one person, excluding wine:
€ = up to €25
€€ = €25–€50
€€€ = over €50

Establishments are open daily unless otherwise stated.

**Eating Out in Venice**
Many restaurants display a set-price *menù turistico* (tourist menu) offering a choice of three or four dishes *(piatti)* for each course; this can be a less expensive way of tasting a number of Venetian specialties.

It can generally be assumed that the bill will include a service charge (ask if uncertain). It is usually 10 per cent (sometimes even as much as 15 per cent).

At any café, bar or snack bar, a seat at a table usually doubles the bill but many of the smaller establishments serve only at the bar and lack even chairs.

**Ae Oche (€–€€)**
A quirky and friendly pizzeria that actually has some good pizzas. With no wood-burning ovens allowed in the city it's not always easy to find a good example but this is one of the best.
**Calle delle Oche, Santa Croce 1552/A 041 524 1161 Lunch, dinner San Stae**

**Ai Corazzieri (€–€€)**
This small but charming restaurant is hidden away behind the Campo Bandiera e Moro and the La Residenza hotel (► 103). Here one of the most delicious Venetian dishes is *tagliolini con cappe sante* (pasta with small scallops in piquant sauce). The kitchen can decide to close early.
**Salizzada dei Corazzieri, Castello 3839 041 528 9859 Lunch, dinner Arsenale**

**Ai Gondolieri (€€€)**
Housed in an old inn, this restaurant specializes in Venetian cooking, particularly meat dishes. It is situated between the Accademia bridge and the Collezione Guggenheim (► 37).
**Camp San Vio, Dorsoduro 366 041 528 6396 Lunch, dinner Accademia**

**Ai Postali (€)**
If it's just a snack you want and you want it late, this is a good option. Located by a quiet canal, this café/bar is a nice place to have a coffee or drink but you can get some good antipasti, sizeable sandwiches or pasta as well.
**Fondameta Rio Marin O Garzotti, Santa Croce 821 041 715 156 Lunch, dinner (open until 1am) Riva di Biasio**

**Al Bacco (€€)**
Get among the locals at this lovely *osteria* (inn) with its typical wood panelling inside or eat in the courtyard garden. Everything is lovingly cooked—good fish and seafood dishes.
**Fondamenta Capuzine, Cannaregio 3054 041 717 493 Lunch, dinner. Closed Mon San Marcuola**

**Al Bottegon (€)**
A wonderful Venetian institution, particularly for lunch. You can get some of the best wine in the city here, the perfect complement to a tasty panini. Lots of bustle and great for people watching.
**Fondamenta Nani, Dorsoduro 992 041 523 0034 Lunch, dinner. Closed Sun Zattere/ Accademia**

**Al Covo (€€€)**
Seriously devoted to fish, be guided by the waiter to get the best out of this experience. Only the best and most fresh of ingredients are used in creating the traditional Venetian recipes. Be sure to reserve ahead.
**Campionello della Pescaria, Castello 3968 041 522 3812 Lunch, dinner. Closed Wed, Thu Arsenale**

**Al Gatto Nero (€€–€€€)**
Off the main tourist trail, this traditional and friendly trattoria offers simply but expertly cooked fresh fish plus a selection of Buranese dishes, including *risotto all buranella* (rice with seafood).
**Fondamenta della Guidecca, Burano 88 041 730 120 Lunch, dinner. Closed Mon Burano LN**

**Algiubagio (€)**
Conveniently placed when waiting for the boat at Fondamente Nuove, and you will have a great view of the cemetry at San Michele. Mingle with the locals for a quick bite—breakfast, pizza and some nice ice cream.
**Fondamente Nove, Cannaregio 5039 041 523 6084 Breakfast–8.30pm Fondamente Nuove**

**Alla Maddelena (€€)**
Linked to the island of Burano by a wooden bridge, Mazzorbo is a different world, little more than a few houses and a couple of trattorias. This one has a wonderful setting and its specialty is wild duck dishes. Reserve a table on Sundays as it is popular with visiting Venetians.
**Mazzorbo 7/C, Mazzorbo 041 523 6084 Lunch only Mazzorbo LN**

**Alla Madonna (€€€)**
One of the oldest restaurants in the city and high on the list of Venetian favourites, especially for business meetings or family celebrations. Lots of space and plenty of typical local dishes including the seafood *ai frutte di mare*. Service can be a bit brusque; there's a quick turnover.
**Calle della Madonna, San Polo 594 041 522 3824 (no reservations) Lunch, dinner. Closed Wed Rialto**

**Alla Rivetta (€)**
It's not easy to find a decent budget range restaurant close to Piazza San Marco but this one can be recommended. Despite its location it does attract locals and serves good, simple fare including tasty seafood.
**Ponte San Provolo, Castello 4625 041 528 7302 Lunch, dinner. Closed Mon San Zaccaria**

**Alla Zucca (€–€€)**
Don't be fooled into thinking this is just another trattoria—there is a twist in the cooking. Some dishes have an Asian theme, others a Mediterranean tang. Mainly vegetarian dishes and hence popular, so reserve.
**Ponte del Megio, Calle del Tintor, Santa Croce 1762 041 524 1570 Lunch, dinner. Closed Sun San Stae**

**Al Mascaron (€–€€)**
Down to earth bar-cum-trattoria with snacks such as the tapas-like *cicheti* but also a menu with pasta, risotto, fish and seafood and salads as well. It's best to reserve.
**Calle Lunga Santa Maria Formosa, Castello 5225 041 522 5995 Lunch, dinner. Closed Sun San Zaccaria**

**Al Ponte (€–€€)**
Its nickname is La Patatina after the renowned large chips served here. Very busy with locals and students and offers hearty food at a good price. Expect seafood risotto and *polpette* (meatballs) on the menu.
**Ponte San Polo, San Polo 2741 041 523 7238 Lunch, dinner. Closed Sun San Tomà**

**Altanella (€€€)**
A pleasant place to go on a trip to the island of Giudecca with its waterside terrace, and quiet setting. Good fresh fish. Service can be slow but it's worth the wait.
**Calle delle Eerbe, Giudecca 268 041 522 7780 Lunch, dinner. Closed Mon, Tue and 2 weeks in Aug Palanca**

**Al Testiere (€€€)**
It may be small but its reputation is huge. Imaginative cooking using local fish blended with delicious spices and herbs. Good cheese and wines.
**Calle del Mondo Novo,**

**Cipriani Restaurants**
Venetian restaurants owe much to the Cipriani family, who has given them a smart yet friendly style. The hotel named after the family is now owned by Sea Containers, which also runs the Orient Express. But the family still runs notable restaurants, although they do now tend to be more expensive and attract the 'in-crowd'.

### Eating Out Tips

Each district has its own little restaurants and there will always be several near each bed-and-breakfast hotel. Tourist menus with dishes at less than the à la carte prices are usually satisfactory but are unlikely to include the more interesting local specialties. In restaurants of any class it is permissible to order pasta as a main course, so reducing the cost of the meal.

**Castello 5801 ☎ 041 522 7220 Lunch, dinner (two dinner sittings). Closed last 2 weeks Dec, first 2 weeks Jan, end of Jul and third week in Aug Rialto**

### Al Vecio Penasa (€)

Not far from San Marco and just off the Riva degli Schiavoni, this is a good spot for a quick coffee, toasted sandwich or even breakfast. It's a bit hectic but the staff are friendly.
**✉ Calle delle Rasse, Castello 4585 ☎ 041 523 7202 Lunch, dinner San Zaccaria**

### Antica Burrana la Corte (€€–€€€)

Set in a converted warehouse, this is something different for Venice—contemporary and minimalist. Good quality food from light bites to full meals.
**✉ Campo San Polo, San Polo 2168 ☎ 041 275 0570 Lunch, dinner San Silvestro**

### Antica Mola (€€€)

Nice setting for a warm night sitting beside the canal or in the garden at the back. Fresh fish of the day and whatever else the chef fancies creating on the day.
**✉ Fondamenta del Ormenisi, Cannaregio 2800 ☎ 041 717 492 Lunch, dinner. Closed Wed San Marcuola**

### Antica Ostaria Ruga Rialto (€)

One of the best for the *cicheti* around, which you can have at the bar or in the room round the back. It's a popular joint with artists and musicians and has occasional live music. Friendly staff.
**✉ Ruga Rialto, San Polo 692 ☎ 041 521 1243 Lunch, dinner Rialto**

### Antiche Carampane (€€€€)

A bit of a secret as it's hard to find but seek it out and you shouldn't be disappointed. Not one for the tourist menu, you will find traditional Venetian dishes (lots of fish) with a modern twist. Be guided by the staff and enjoy.
**✉ Rio terra Carampane, San Polo 1911 ☎ 041 524 0165 Lunch, dinner. Closed Sun, Mon San Silvestro**

### Antico Martini (€€€)

One of the city's most sophisiticated restaurants and frequented by the high society set. Classic dishes such as *fegato all Veneziana con polenta* (liver with onions and polenta). Sumptuous desserts and fine wines.
**✉ Campo San Fantin, San Marco 1983 ☎ 041 522 4121 Lunch, dinner. Closed Tue, dinner only Nov, Dec Giglio**

### Bistrot de Venise (€€–€€€)

An atmospheric setting in a 16th-century palazzo and the dishes match the period. Popular with poets and the artistic crowd and there are occasional readings and exhibitions. Good wine list.
**✉ Calle de Fabbri, San Marco 4685 ☎ 041 523 6651 Lunch, dinner Rialto**

### Busa alla Torre (€€)

Take a break from the glass shops with a tasty fish meal or a Murano island specialty. Well known for its crab dishes, such as fried *moeche* (little shore crabs). Good homemade pasta, too.
**✉ Campo Santo Stefano, Murano 3 ☎ 041 739 662 Lunch only Murano 41, 42**

### Casin di Nobili (€€–€€€)

This, the 'little house of the noble people' is very popular and does get busy. Mostly used for its pizzas, there are a good range of alternatives on offer. You can sit out in the pretty garden in summer.
**✉ Campo San Barnaba, Dorsoduro 2765 ☎ 041 241 1841 Lunch, dinner. Closed Sun Ca' Rezzonica**

**Corte Sconta (€€€)**
This is an all-time favourite Venetian restaurant and it's always busy. It's also off the main tourist drag and the cooking is first rate. Particularly noted for its fresh fish and seafood classics but the pastas and traditional puddings are also excellent.
**✉ Calle di Pestrin, Castello 3886 ☎ 041 522 7024 🕔 Lunch, dinner. Closed Jan to early Feb, mid-Jul to mid-Aug ⛴ Arsenale**

**Da Alberto (€€)**
This is the real thing—an authentic Venetian bar-cum-restaurant serving snacks *cicheti* style, including tasty *sarde in saor* (sweet and sour sardines) and *seppie in umido* (stewed cuttlefish); also good dried cod. Best to reserve a table.
**✉ Calle Giacinto Gallina, Cannaregio 5401 ☎ 041 523 8153 🕔 Lunch, dinner. Closed Sun and mid-Jul to mid-Aug ⛴ Fondemente Nuove**

**Da Fiore (€€€)**
Much sought after by the Venetian glitterati makes it hard to get a table at this top restaurant and it's not easy to find either. The use of ultra fresh ingredients produces mouthwatering high quality fish dishes and beautifully sauced hand-rolled pastas. One of the best wine cellars in the city.
**✉ Calle del Scaleter, San Polo 2202/A ☎ 041 721 308 🕔 Lunch, dinner. Closed Sun, Mon ⛴ San Stae/San Silvestro**

**Da Ignazio (€€–€€€)**
This courtyard restaurant is a great setting; by day there is shade, or eat under romantic Venetian lighting at night. The food is regional Italian, and it's a good place to take children to as the service is quick.
**✉ Calle dei Saoneri, San Polo 2749 ☎ 041 523 4852 🕔 Lunch, dinner. Closed Sat ⛴ San Tomà**

**Dal Pampo/Osteria Sant'Elena (€€–€€€)**
One of the most friendly restaurants around mainly due to the welcoming owner, Pampo. Good wholesome cooking and full bodied wines. Primarily a local's place but you will be made very welcome.
**✉ Calle Generale Chinotto, Castello 24 ☎ 041 520 8419 🕔 Lunch, dinner. Closed Thu and 1 week in May and Aug ⛴ Sant'Elena**

**Da Remigio (€€)**
One of the more authentic trattoria and as a result popular, so you will need to reserve a table. Good honest fare, excellent antipasti and the freshest of fish.
**✉ Salizzada dei Greci, Castello 3416 ☎ 041 523 0089 🕔 Lunch, dinner. Closed Mon dinner, Tue, Jan and 2 weeks during Jul or Aug ⛴ San Zaccaria**

**Da Renato (€€)**
This is real down-to-earth eating, no frills but a place to get a hearty soup or stew, good snacks and a tasty selection of desserts. The clientele are fun—look for the gondoliers.
**✉ Rio Terra Seconda, San Polo 2245/A ☎ 041 7524 1922 🕔 Lunch, dinner ⛴ San Stae**

**Da Sergio (€)**
A good value place frequented by locals—always a good bet for an authentic meal and old-fashioned cooking. Helps to know a little Italian.
**✉ Calle del Dose, Castello 5870/A ☎ 041 528 5153 🕔 Lunch, dinner. Closed Sun ⛴ San Zaccaria**

**Do Forni (€€€)**
Popular with both tourists and locals alike, there are two dining rooms here. One is rustic, the other has Murano glass chandliers and opulence. Huge menu

**More Tips**
There are some 300 restaurants in the city. Some close in the low seasons and many shut on Sundays and Mondays, except those in hotels, and the grander of these serve food suitable to their style, often out of doors in summer. Particularly recommended are the restaurants in the Gritti Palace (► 102), the Danieli (► 101) and the Londra Palace (► 103).

### Who was Harry?

The famous Harry's Bar was founded in 1931 and there is a legend surrounding its inception. It is said that an American known only as 'Harry' remarked to a hotel barman that he couldn't find a decent bar in Venice. The barman, Guiseppe Cipriani, decided to change that, arranged financial backing and bought an old rope store near San Marco and opened the now famous bar. Always popular with the rich and famous, Ernest Hemingway spent a good deal of time propping up the bar, as do today's celebrities and countless tourists.

ranging from classic Italian to international dishes.
**✉ Calle dei Specchieri, San Marco 468 ☎ 041 523 0663 ⌚ Lunch, dinner ⛴ Vallaresso (San Marco)**

### Dona Onesta (€)

The 'Honest Woman' produces fine food at very reasonable prices. Sadly its secret seems to be out and it is now necessary to reserve a table as the dining room is small. Nice quiet spot overlooking the canal.
**✉ Calle della Donna Onesta, Dorsoduro ☎ 041 710 586 ⌚ Lunch, dinner. Closed Sun ⛴ San Tomà**

### Fiaschetteria Toscana (€€€)

Established in 1956 and despite the name the menu includes classic Venetian dishes and excellent seafood, all lovingly prepared. Great selection of wines from Tuscany.
**✉ Salizzada San Gionvanni Grisostomo, Cannaregio 5719 ☎ 041 528 5281 ⌚ Lunch, dinner. Closed Mon dinner, Tue and 3 weeks in Jul ⛴ Rialto**

### Florian (€)

Cafés have long played an important part in Venetian life, particularly in the exchange of news and gossip. Florian, opened in 1720, is expensive but a great place for people watching. In cold weather, the interior of Florian—all faded plush and 19th-century murals—is magnificent.
**✉ Piazza San Marco, San Marco 56–59 ☎ 041 520 5641 ⌚ Coffee, teas light snacks until midnight. Closed Wed in Dec–end Feb ⛴ Vallaresso (San Marco)**

### Gam Gam (€€–€€€)

If you want to experience authentic Venetian Jewish cooking this restaurant in the Ghetto is a good bet. Fully kosher, the diverse menu offers dishes from spaghetti to couscous (with a choice of meat, fish or vegetable sauce).Tasty *bourekas* and falafels as well.
**✉ Fondamenta Cannaregio, Cannaregio 1122 ☎ 041 715 284 ⌚ Lunch, dinner. Closed Sat ⛴ Guglie**

### Harry's Bar (€€€)

This was the original Cipriani establishment, a popular haunt of Ernest Hemingway. It still has an air of the 1930s and there is often so much to watch indoors that nobody looks at the view through the opaque windows. The food is delicious, if expensive. Try the *tagliolini verdi gratinati* (green pasta with chopped ham in a cheese sauce) and a jug of chilled Soave white wine from the Veneto.
**✉ Calle Vallaresso, San Marco 1323 ☎ 041 528 577 ⌚ Lunch, dinner ⛴ Vallaresso (San Marco)**

### Harry's Dolci (€€€)

Over on Giudecca island, the same management has a restaurant—originally designed as a tearoom—next to its own bakery. Serves much the same sort of food as Harry's Bar, but with emphasis on puddings and cakes. There are wonderful views from the outside tables, siutated right beside the water .
**✉ Fondamento San Biagio, Guidecca 773 ☎ 041 522 4844 ⌚ Lunch, dinner. Closed Tue Nov–end Apr ⛴ Palanca**

### Il Giardino di Giada (€€)

Don't be put off by the exterior, it's lovely inside and the food's pretty good, too. One of the best Chinese restaurants in the city serving high quality food to locals and visitors alike. Try the tasty fresh fish dishes.
**✉ Calle dei Botteri, San Polo 1659 ☎ 041 721 673 ⌚ Lunch, dinner ⛴ Rialto**

**Il Refolo (€€)**
In a quiet corner close to the church and by the canal, this restaurant, the 'Sea Breeze', is a popular spot for first-rate pizza, pasta or salad. If you're hungry there are more substantial main courses to be washed down with some good house wine. And you may be tempted by the scrumptious desserts.
**✉ Campo San Giacomo dell'Olio, Santa Croce 1459 ☎ 041 524 0016 ⌚ Lunch, dinner. Closed Mon and Tue lunch ⛴ San Stae**

**La Caravella (€€€)**
This is one of the two restaurants in the Saturnia hotel and this one resembles a Venetian galley. It's a bit over the top but the food's good and the experience fun. Classic Venetian cooking with international twist.
**✉ Calle Larga (Viale) XXII Marzo, San Marco 2398 ☎ 041 520 8901 ⌚ Lunch, dinner ⛴ Giglio**

**La Colonna (€€–€€€)**
Small, intimate and nice for a romantic dinner for two. One of a new style of restaurants giving Venetian cooking a contemporary edge and the result is excellent. Great desserts.
**✉ Campiello del Pestrin, Cannaregio 5329 ☎ 041 522 9641 ⌚ Lunch, dinner. Closed Mon and 2 weeks in Aug ⛴ San Tomà**

**L'Incontro (€€€)**
For something a bit different, come here for the Sardinian cooking. The tastes are stronger and the dishes wholesome, reflecting the nature of the south. Try the classic dish *seadas* (sweet ravioli covered in hot honey). The southern wines are also good.
**✉ Campo Santa Margherita, Dorsoduro 3062/A ☎ 041 721 673 ⌚ Lunch, dinner ⛴ Rialto**

**Locanda Cipriani (€€€)**
Another and the most delectable endowment by the Cipriani family is on the island of Torcello to the northeast of Venice. Its particular joy is lunch outside in the walled garden with the tower of the cathedral just beyond. The matchless cuisine makes for an unforgettable experience.
**✉ Piazza Santa Fosca, Torcello 29 ☎ 041 730 150 ⌚ Lunch dinner. Closed Tue Nov–end Mar ⛴ Torcello LN**

**Locanda Montin (€€€)**
Among the best-known garden restaurants, it is cheerful and cosy inside when too cold for eating outdoors. It is difficult to find in a quiet and charming district near the Campo San Barnaba, but so popular that reservations are essential.
**✉ Fondamento di Borgo, Dorsoduro 1147 ☎ 041 522 7151 ⌚ Lunch, dinner. Closed Wed ⛴ Ca' Rezzonico/Accademia**

**Mistra (€–€€)**
This restaurant in a converted warehouse in Giudecca is full of locals. It is a comfortable place, serving good fresh fish and seafood, eaten while admiring lovely views over the lagoon. A bit off the tourist trail but well signposted.
**✉ Fondamenta San Giacomo, Giudecca 212/A ☎ 041 522 0743 ⌚ Lunch, dinner. Closed Mon dinner and Tue ⛴ Redentore**

**Nico (€)**
Ever popular *gelataria* (ice-cream shop) in a lovely spot on the waterfront to enjoy an ice cream looking out over the water to Giudecca. For a succulent change try the *gianduitto* (a chocolate and hazelnut ice topped with whipped cream) or for the more weight conscious try the frozen yogurt varieties. Also juices and snacks.

**Garden Restaurants**
Gardens are much more unusual than water in Venice, so restaurants with the former rightly make much of eating beneath a vine in a sun-dappled courtyard or under Venetian lanterns at night.

**Eating by the Water**
Waterside meals are a particular Venetian pleasure and these can be enjoyed on the Zattere or by quiet canals. There is a row of relatively cheap and cheerful pizzerie lining the *fondamenta* at this end of the Zattere, with tables on wooden platforms built out over the water. Here, beside the bridge over the San Trovaso canal, pizza with wine followed by ice cream and coffee provides an excuse for sitting an hour or so in the sun, and is not so expensive.

**Fondementa Zattere, Dorsoduro 922 041 522 5293 Lunch, dinner. Closed Thu Zattere**

**Osteria Al Bacareto (€€)**
As an alternative to looking at water or boats, the passing throng is also a Venetian pleasure and some restaurants have tables out in a campo. Among many, cheerful, unpretentious Al Bacareto is a typically Venetian trattorie. You can have a full meal or snack.
**Calle Crosera, San Marco 3447 041 528 9336 Lunch, dinner. Closed Sat and Sun Sant'Angelo/San Samuele**

**Osteria Al Bomba (€€)**
Popular with gondoliers taking their lunch break for its good value and tasty snacks. Although main dishes are usually of fish, this restaurant is a good bet for vegetarians, with a selection cooked in imaginative ways. Look beyond the rather plain surroundings and it's worth the visit.
**Calle del Oca, Cannaregio 4297/98 041 241 1146 Lunch, dinner. Closed Wed Ca' d'oro**

**Ostaria Boccadoro (€€–€€€)**
Tucked away this is a popular spot for well-to-do Venetians. Seafood is at the forefront of the menu—you can get clams or oysters or try some of the raw fish dishes popular here including tuna. There's a good wine list, with particular emphasis on wines from Sardinia.
**Campo Widman, Cannaregio 5405/A 041 521 1021 Lunch, dinner. Closed Mon Fondamente Nuove**

**Osteria Da Rioba (€€–€€€)**
A relative newcomer that is gaining a following among the younger Venetian set, it is named after the Moorish statue in the nearby Palazzo Mastelli. Minimalist in comparison to the usual *osteria*, its emphasis is on Venetian classics, such as rabbit stew and fish dishes.
**Fondamenta della Misericordia, Cannaregio 2553 041 524 4379 Lunch, dinner. Closed Mon Madonna dell'Orto**

**Osteria Oliva Nera (€€€)**
Venetian classics meet modern cooking; this is among several restaurants in the city now cooking traditional food with a modern edge. Dishes include succulent lamb cooked in thyme and octopus salad. Lovely tempting desserts. Add some nice staff and this makes for a good experience all round.
**Calle della Madonna, Castello 3417/18 041 522 2170 Lunch, dinner. Closed Wed and Thu San Zaccaria**

**Paolin (€)**
Located in one of Venice's loveliest squares, this is one of the city's best cafés and *gelateria* (ice-cream shop) and one of the oldest. Nice in summer to sit at one of the outside tables and try some of the great summer fruit ice creams—strawberry, melon, lemon or apricot.
**Campo Santo Stefano, San Marco 2962 041 522 5576 Lunch, dinner Closed Mon in winter Accademia, San Samuele**

**Pizzeria (€)**
Sometimes you just want

that basic well-cooked tasty pizza and you can get one here; in fact, it's one of the best in the city. Very popular so you may well have to wait but there's plenty to watch as they prepare the pizzas in front of you.
**✉ Salizzada S. Guistina, Castello 2907/A ☎ 041 520 4198 ⌚ Lunch, dinner. Closed Wed and Thu 🚢 S. Guistina**

**Quadri (€–€€€)**
It may not be as famous as Florian (► 96) but it is equally as theatrical and has umpteen chandeliers and mirrors, creating a stunning effect. You can have a pricey coffee or a full meal (some good vegetarian options) overlooking the piazza.
**✉ Piazza San Marco, San Marco 120/124 ☎ 041 522 2105 ⌚ Closed Mon in winter 🚢 Vallaresso (San Marco)**

**Trattoria da Fiore (€€–€€€)**
If you just want a quick bite, the *cicheti* here is excellent and can be eaten standing at the bar with a glass of wine among the locals. If you want more take a table and feast off *fritto misto* (mixed fried fish) or try the spaghetti with seafood.
**✉ Calle delle Botteghe, San Marco 3460 ☎ 041 523 5310 ⌚ Lunch, dinner. Closed Tue 🚢 San Samuele**

**Trattoria San Tomà (€–€€)**
Eat here as much for the area, close to some of the finest buildings in Venice—Santa Maria Gloriosa dei Frari and the Scoula Grande dei San Rocco–as for the excellent choice of pizza or main course.
**✉ Calle delle Botteghe, San Marco 3460 ☎ 041 523 5310 ⌚ Lunch, dinner. Closed Tue 🚢 San Samuele**

**Vecio Fritolin (€)**
Lovely atmosphere in an old fashioned trattoria, which is popular with locals for a snack or an excellent fish dish usually fried or flame grilled. Basics such as polenta, beans and pasta all of a high standard.
**✉ Calle della Regina, Santa Croce 2262 ☎ 041 522 2881 ⌚ Lunch, dinner. Closed Sun dinner, Mon and Aug 🚢 San Stae**

**Vini da Arturo (€€€)**
If you've had enough fish or you have a preference for meat, this is one of the few restaurants in Venice to concentrate on meat dishes. In the pleasant wood panelled dining room you'll find mainly locals dining on succulent steaks and veal and you will be assured of a friendly welcome.
**✉ Rio Terrà degli Assassini, San Marco 3656 ☎ 041 528 6974 ⌚ Closed Sun 🚢 Sant'Angelo**

**Vini da Gigio (€€)**
The perfect setting for an atmospheric dinner, in two intimate, rustic dining rooms by the canal. This is the one for the authentic and traditional home-cooked Venetian meal. The menu is seafood based but meat and game also feature. Seasonal is the key here with the freshest of ingredients used.
**✉ Fondamenta San Felice, Castello 3628/A ☎ 041 528 5140 ⌚ Closed Sun dinner, Mon and 3 weeks in Aug 🚢 Ca' d'Oro**

**Vivaldi (€)**
Set among the busy shopping streets of San Polo, this is a quiet cosy refuge to relax and have a simple meal. Snacks and a drink are available but there are a few tables at which to have a more substantial meal. The *grigliata di pesce* (mixed fish grill) is a good choice.
**✉ Calle della Madonnetta, San Polo 1457 ☎ 041 523 8185 ⌚ Lunch, dinner 🚢 San Silvestro**

**Where to Eat**
In addition to the usual Italian eateries (*osterie, ristoranti, trattorie* and *gelaterie*) Venice has one of its own—the *bàcaro*. It is a small bar that sells wine by the glass, which is accompanied by a selection of little snacks, *cicheti*, not unlike Spanish tapas. The *enoteca* (wine bar) seen throughout Italy may also serve food.

# Venice

**Prices**
The price indications below are for a double room per night:
€ = under €100
€€ = €100–€200
€€€ = €200–€280
€€€€ = over €280

There can be a marked difference in the price for a room in high or low season, which can be reduced by as much as half. The prices here are given for high season. This runs from the week before Easter until the end of June and then from early September until early November. July and August are cheaper as people choose to stay at the beach rather than the stifling confines of the city. However, these months are still very busy and packed with tourists on day trips. Remember the city will be more expensive and very busy during the carnival in February (► 116).

**Accademia-Villa Maravege (€€€)**
This is a 17th-century house in its own garden at the junction of two canals, just off the Grand Canal, which once housed the Russian Embassy. Its position remains idyllic, particularly when the wisteria is in bloom, and it is convenient for districts away from the tourist trails. It's 37 rooms are nicely furnished but can be rather small.
**✉ Fondamenta Balloni, Dorsoduro 1058 ☎ 041 523 7846; www.pensioneaccademia.it ⛴ Accademia**

**Agli Alboretti (€€)**
Only 19 rooms in this hotel and some are a bit on the small side but it's pretty and has a pleasant courtyard where breakfast is served in the summer. It is very popular and you will need to reserve well in advance. Nice restaurant and good locale.
**✉ Rio Terrà Foscarini, Dorsoduro 884 ☎ 041 523 0058; www.agliaboretti.com ⛴ Accademia**

**American (€€–€€€)**
Recently refurbished, the rooms are now light and airy. The hotel is located by a pretty and quiet canal and has the added bonus of a garden. A good choice away from the crowds. The staff are helpful and even arrange a babysitting service and reservations for tours.
**✉ Fondamenta Bragadin, Dorsoduro 628 ☎ 041 520 4733; www.hotelamerican.com ⛴ Accademia**

**Ateneo (€€)**
This quiet hotel, tucked away in a hidden alley, is near the beautiful newly restored Teatro La Fenice, the smart shops and pleasant squares.
**✉ Calle Minelli, Campo San Fantin, San Marco 1876 ☎ 041 520 0777; www.ateneo.it ⛴ Vallaresso (San Marco)**

**Bauer Grünwald (€€€€)**
For truly stupendous rooftop and balcony views you can't beat this luxury hotel. It's in two halves, a modern hotel with most of the rooms and the sumptuous 18th-century palazzo with wonderful antiques, Murano chandeliers and glorious fabrics. With 196 rooms and 60 suites this is the ultimate —saunas, Jacuzzis, health club and superb dining.
**✉ Campo San Moise, San Marco 1459 ☎ 041 520 7022; www.bauervenezia.it ⛴ Vallaresso (San Marco)**

**Bel Sito e Berlino (€€)**
Those wishing to be in the social mainstream but cannot afford the Gritti Palace (► 102) would do well to choose the Bel Sito, just a short step away and opposite a peculiar Venetian church with a façade carved with battle rather than Biblical scenes.
**✉ Santa Maria del Giglio, San Marco 2517 ☎ 041 522 3365; www.hotelbelsito.info ⛴ Giglio**

**Calcina (€€)**
Another fine view of water—in this case the Canale Giudecca—is from the Calcina, the small hotel on the Zattere, where Ruskin stayed while writing *The Stones of Venice*. The 29 rooms are attractively furnished with period touches. Two nice terraces. Good value and one of the

best settings for the price.
✉ **Fondamenta Zattere ai Gesuati, Dorsoduro 779** ☎ **041 520 6466; www.lacalcina.com** 🚢 **Zattere**

**Ca' Maria Adele (€€€€)**
Ideally placed near the beautiful church of Santa Maria della Salute and the vaparetto stop, this is luxury personified. With only 7 rooms and 7 suites you choose your themed room from cosy to Oriental.
✉ **Rio Terrà dei Catecumeni, Dorsoduro 111** ☎ **041 520 3078; www.camariadele.it** 🚢 **Salute**

**Cavalletto e Doge Orseolo (€€€)**
Close to Piazzo San Marco, this 107-room hotel has been in business for two centuries. Its rooms are elaborately furnished in Venetian style yet provide modern comforts. Some rooms overlook the canal.
✉ **Calle Cavelleto, San Marco 1107** ☎ **041 520 0955; www.sanmarcohotels.com** 🚢 **Vallaresso (San Marco)**

**Cipriani (€€€€)**
This ranks among one of the world's greatest hotels and it has a price to match. If it's luxury, privacy and impeccable service you want, you will get it here on the island of Giudecca. It has a magnificent open-air swimming pool, a miraculous cure for fatigue after a long day's sightseeing in the city. Other facilities include gym, beauty centre, tennis courts and the famous Cipriani restaurant (► 97). Shuttle boat service to San Marco.
✉ **Giudecca 10** ☎ **041 520 7744; www.hotelcirpirani.it** 🚢 **Zitelle**

**Danieli (€€€€)**
Guests here have included some of the city's most famous visitors—Dickens, Wagner and Proust among them—and the original building has atmosphere and sumptuous style in its public rooms. Superb service and good food. You should reserve a room in the old building rather than the newer annexe. There are a total of 230 rooms and 11 suites to choose from.
✉ **Riva degli Schiavoni 4196** ☎ **041 522 6480; www.luxurycollection.com** 🚢 **San Zaccaria**

**Des Bains (€€€–€€€€)**
The doom-laden film *Death in Venice* was made here and this Lido hotel exudes a suitably stately gloom. The striking art deco building may have seen better days, but it is still as popular as ever. The 291 rooms are well-equipped and the attractive grounds have a swimming pool, tennis courts, gym and sauna and access to a private beach.
✉ **Lungomare Marconi, Lido 17** ☎ **041 526 592; www.starwoodhotels.com** 🚢 **Lido Santa Maria Elisabetta**

**Fiorita (€)**
Among the most simple pensioni, the pretty Fiorita is well-sited just north of Santo Stefano. It is welcoming, clean and uncomplicated; the 10 comfortable rooms (8 with private bath) have beamed ceilings.
✉ **Campiello Nuovo, San Marco 3457/A** ☎ **041 523 4754; www.locandafiorita.com** 🚢 **Accademia/Sant'Angelo**

**Flora (€€)**
Some visitors choose the 44-roomed Flora, largely because of its lush, secluded garden and because it is conveniently close to fashionable shops. Some rooms are rather cramped, varying in size considerably. Friendly and helpful staff.
✉ **Calle Bergamaschi, San Marco 2283/A** ☎ **041 520 5844; www.hotelflora.com** 🚢 **Giglio**

**Availability**
It is always best to reserve a room before arriving in Venice. Accommodation levels in the city have risen considerably since the mid-1990s, but the demand has increased equally and it can be difficult to find rooms at busy times. Many hotels will no longer take large groups, having been discouraged by the stag and hen parties that have plagued the city.

**What to Expect**
There are about 200 hotels in Venice and, this being Italy, most of them are well run. A few may have become slatternly through over-confidence induced by a nonstop flow of package tourists, but their principal handicap is age. A medieval palace, religious institution or merchant's house cannot be converted into a modern hotel with identical bedrooms, although ruthless use of steel joists has opened up many a spacious lobby behind a Renaissance façade. Thus the same hotel is likely to offer both large and lofty bedrooms commanding magnificent views and dark poky rooms overlooking a dank ventilation well or an alley. If a particular hotel is known to command fine views, suitable rooms can usually be reserved at an extra charge.

**Foresteria Valdese (€)**
This is a hostel with a difference. Housed in the magnifiencent Palazzo Cavagnis near the lively Campo Santa Maria Formosa, it is run by the Waldensian and Methodist church in Venice. Accommodation ranges from dormitory beds (only available for groups by reservation) to comfortable doubles (75 beds in total). Concerts and cultural events are hosted in the private rooms.
**☒ Calle della Madonetta, Castello 5170 ☏ 041 528 6797; www.diaconivaldese.org/venezia/foresteria ⛴ Rialto**

**Girogione (€€€)**
Based in a 15th-century palazzo and a newer building, the 70 rooms are decorated in period style, all with great attention to detail. There is a flower-filled courtyard for taking breakfast, complete with lily pond.
**☒ Campo Santi Apostoli, Cannregio 4587 ☏ 041 522 5810; www.hotelgiorgione.com ⛴ Ca' d'Oro**

**Grand Hotel Excelsior Palace (€€€)**
This is a turn-of-the-20th-century mock Moorish architectural fantasy with 197 rooms and suites, half of which overlook the sea. It still attracts the celebrities during the Film Festival and exudes style. Its main pull is the private beach with its luxurious Moorish-style cabanas. Facilities include two restaurants, beauty therapies, outdoor pool, watersports and tennis courts. Launch service connects to San Marco.
**☒ Lungomre Marconi, Lido 41 ☏ 041 526 0201; www.starwoodhotels.com ⛴ Lido Santa Maria Elisabetta**

**Gritti Palace (€€€€)**
This must be the queen of all the Venetian grand hotels—in fact the present Queen Elizabeth of Britain has chosen it as her Venetian base. It was built as a palazzo in the 15th century and sumptuously converted while retaining its original style. In summer, its principal delight is the open-air Terrazza del Doge, where meals are served beside the Grand Canal. A courtesy launch is provided to take you to the hotel group's facilities on the Lido.
**☒ Santa Maria del Giglio, San Marco 2467 ☏ 041 794 611; www.starwoodhotels.com ⛴ Giglio**

**Iris (€€)**
In business since the 1930s the Flora family hotel was refurbished in the late 1990s. Eighteen of the simply furnished 24 rooms have a private bathroom and all have air-conditioning. The highlight of this hotel is the pretty garden and the restaurant Al Giardinetto that serves excellent pizza.
**☒ Fondementa dei Forner, San Polo 2910/A ☏ 041 522 2882; www.venice-hotel.irishotel.com; ⛴ San Tomà**

**La Fenice e Des Artistes (€€)**
This hotel is quite charmingly furnished and close to the newly restored Teatro La Fenice. Some of the 67 rooms have balconies. The La Taverna restaurant serves classic Venetian dishes and

there is a nice courtyard area for breakfast.
**✉ Campiello Fenice, San Marco 1936 ☎ 041 523 2333; www.fenicehotels.com 🚢 Giglio**

**La Galleria (€€)**
A simple, old-fashioned style of hotel that's welcoming and comfortable and good value considering its prime location close to the Grand Canal and the Gallerie dell'Accademia. Twelve rooms in all but reserve well in advance to get one of the larger ones overlooking the canal.
**✉ Campo della Carità, Dorsoduro 878/A ☎ 041 523 2489; www.hotelgalleria.it 🚢 Accademia**

**La Residenza (€–€€)**
This is another palace where the Gritti family lived, hidden away in a campo off the Riva degli Schiavoni. This intensely Venetian pensione has a magnificent salon with paintings, plasterwork and chandeliers, off which passages lead to the 15 comfortable bedrooms.
**✉ Bandiera e Moro, Castello 3608 ☎ 041 528 315; www.venicelaresidenza.com 🚢 Arsenale**

**Locanda Antica Venezia (€€)**
Just a stone's throw from Piazza San Marco and not far from the Teatro La Fenice, this friendly, good value hotel is located down a small alley just off the shopping street, Frezzeria. Located on the third floor of the 16th-century residence, don't be put off by the entrace hall—the hotel itself is well decorated and has a lovely beamed sitting area and rooftop terrace, with views of the Campanile, for breakfast or drinks.
**✉ Piscina di Frezzeria, San Marco 1672 ☎ 041 520 8320; www.hotelanticavenezia.com 🚢 Vallaresso (San Marco)**

**Locanda Ca' Foscari (€)**
This is a good bet if you are on a limited budget. A homey feel to this place, more like a guest house than a hotel. Not all the 11 rooms have their own bathroom but everything is clean and bright. It is well situated near the church of Santa Maria Gloriosa dei Frari and does a good breakfast.
**✉ Calle della Frescada, Dorsoduro 3887/B ☎ 041 520 8320; www.locandacafoscari.com 🚢 San Tomà**

**Londra Palace (€€€–€€€€)**
This is one of the hotels in a prime position along the Riva degli Schiavoni overlooking the Basin of San Marco. Refurbished in the late 1990s its 53 rooms and suites and public rooms retain their former old style tranquility. Nice roof terrace and a good restaurant.
**✉ Riva degli Schiavoni, Castello 4171 ☎ 041 520 0533; www.slh.com/londra 🚢 San Zaccaria**

**Luna Baglioni (€€€)**
Venice's oldest hotel has had an overhaul. Its position near the Piazza San Marco is convenient for exploring the city and the views from some of the 100 rooms are excellent and all are well-equipped. The public areas are sumptuous and the restaurant offers Venetian specialties.
**✉ Calle dell'Ascensione, San Marco 1243 ☎ 041 528 9840; www.baglionihotels.com 🚢 Vallaresso (San Marco)**

**Marconi (€€–€€€)**
You will have to get in quick to reserve one of the two rooms with a Grand Canal view but the other 24 do have an advantage—peace and quiet. This was considered an exclusive hotel in the 1930s and it has managed to retain some of

**Venetian Apartments**
If you are looking for a different style of accommodation, British-based company, Venetian Apartments, offers more than 100 aparments in central Venice and on the island of Giudecca for rent. They have been in business for 16 years and are very knowledgeable about Venice. Top of the agenda are historic and luxurious apartments in *palazzi* and former aristocrats' residences. Some are on the Grand Canal, others in quieter secretive and evocative locations. All are beautifully furnished. They vary considerably in size but all are fully equipped for self-catering (✉ 403 Parkway House, Sheen Lane, London SW14 8LS ☎ 020 8878 1130; www.venice-rentals.com).

**Lido Hotels**
Two gigantic relics of the heyday of the Lido, Des Bains (► 101) and Excelsior (► 102) are hotels designed for rich pre-1914 families. Both come alive during the Mostra del Cinema Venezia (Venice Film Festival, ► 116), which is concentrated on the Lido, and both are as expensive as one would expect from their glamorous associations.

that pre-war charm. Take a close-up view of the Rialto bridge over a coffee from one of the outdoor tables.
**✉ Riva del Vin, San Polo 729 ☎ 041 522 2068; www.hotelmarconi.it ⛴ Rialto**

### Metropole (€€€)
Another hotel on the Riva degli Schiavoni with a fine view of the Basin of San Marco. Comfortable and well-run, the 70 spacious rooms are nicely decorated with paintings and furnished with anitques and period furniture.
**✉ Riva degli Schiavoni, Castello 4199 ☎ 041 520 5044; www.hotelmetropole.com ⛴ Vallaresso (San Marco)**

### Novecento (€€–€€€)
A nine-room boutique hotel of a type now becoming increasingly popular in Venice. A fusion of traditional and Middle Eastern design is reflected in the furnishings. The rooms have every comfort and smart Phillipe Starck bathrooms. Tiny courtyard and garden where breakfast is served when the weather is good.
**✉ Calle delle Dose, Campo San Maurizio, San Marco 2683 ☎ 041 241 3765; www.locandanovecento.it ⛴ Giglio**

### Ostello di Venezia (€)
A well-run youth hostel on Guidecca Island with 260 beds. Cheap and basic, it's one of the few ways to have an inexpensive stay in Venice. It is best to send a written reservation especially if you are planning to come in the summer. There's an 11pm curfew.
**✉ Fondamenta delle Zitelle, Guidecca 86 ☎ 041 523 8211; www.ostellionline.org ⛴ Zitelle**

### Pausania (€€)
This hotel is on a quiet canal and located in the former 14th-century residence of a member of the Venetian aristocracy. The rooms are a good size and all are well-equipped. The hotel has the advantage of a big veranda—overlooking a garden—where breakfast is served.
**✉ San Barnaba, Dorsoduro 2824 ☎ 041 522 2083; www.hotelpausania.it ⛴ Ca' Rezzónica**

### Pensione Bucintoro (€€)
One of the best views from a hotel in Venice. All the bedroom windows overlook the Riva degli Schiavoni, the Basin of San Marco and the island of San Giorgio, the Salute and the Doges' Palace beyond. Run by a delightful family, it is cosy rather than smart. Not all bedrooms have private bathrooms so specify what you want when making a reservation. Closed in December and January.
**✉ Riva San Biagio, Castello 2135 ☎ 041 522 3240; fax 041 523 5224 ⛴ Arsenale**

### Pensione Seguso (€€)
This long-established and atmospheric, family-run pensione is situated on the Zattere, facing across the shipping channel to Giudecca island. Most of its 36 traditionally furnished rooms have canal views. You can take breakfast on the pleasant terrace.
**✉ Zattere, Dorsoduro 779 ☎ 041 528 6858; www.pensioneseguso.com ⛴ Zattere**

**San Cassiano-Ca' Favretto (€€–€€€)**
In a converted 14th-century palazzo on the opposite side of the Grand Canal from the glorious Ca' d'Oro palace. Half the 35 rooms face the Grand Canal, the rest a side canal. Nice place to stay if you want something quieter.
**✉ Calle della Rosa, Santa Croce 2232 ☎ 041 524 1768; www.sancassiano.it ⛴ San Stae**

**San Clemente Palace (€€€€)**
This is the latest 200-room luxury hotel in Venice located on the island of San Clemente. The complex is the result of the restoration of the monastery built in the second half of the 17th century, and the careful modernization has succeeded in retaining the historic ambience. It is set in 1.5ha (4 acres) of park and gardens, and facilities include swimming pool, tennis courts, a spa and beauty club, three-hole practise golf course plus bars and three restaurants. Access is by private launch.
**✉ Isola di San Clemente, San Marco 1 ☎ 041 244 5001; www.thi.it ⛴ Private launch**

**San Fantin (€€)**
A quiet hotel close to the Teatro La Fenice, it was once headquarters for the Venetians' rebellion against Austrian rule in 1848. Its façade is decorated with guns and cannonballs. It has been managed by the same family for over 46 years and they will look after you with great care.
**✉ Campiello Fenice, San Marco 1930/A ☎ 041 523 1401; www.sanfantin.com ⛴ Giglio**

**San Moisè (€€€)**
A rather splendid 16th-century Venetian building is home to this hotel set by the canal with a pleasant, shaded courtyard. The 16 rooms feature Murano glass chandeliers, elaborate draperies and antiques while offering modern facilities.
**✉ Piscina San Moisè, San Marco 2058 ☎ 041 520 3755; www.hotelsanmoise.com ⛴ Vallaresso (San Marco)/Giglio**

**San Samuele (€)**
A budget hotel with a good location near the San Samuele vaparetto stop. Friendly, basic but clean and well run. Most of the 10 rooms have shared bath.
**✉ Salizzada San Samuele, San Marco 3358 ☎ 041 522 8045; fax 041 522 8045 ⛴ San Samuele**

**Santo Stefano (€€€)**
Housed in a 15th-century watchtower, this hotel is popular with business clients and tourists alike. In addition to attractive, elegant rooms, each bathroom has a Jacuzzi and Turkish bath.
**✉ Campo San Stefano, San Marco 2957 ☎ 041 520 0166; www.hotelsantostefanovenezia.com ⛴ Accademia**

**Scandinavia (€€€)**
Located in one of Venice's nicest squares, this hotel is comfortable and spacious, with the furnishings reflecting the 18th century. The 37 rooms are well-equipped but be aware the prices go up for those overlooking the square.
**✉ Campo Santa Maria Formosa, Castello 5240 ☎ 041 522 3507; www.scandinaviahotel.com ⛴ Rialto**

**A Good Night's Sleep**
Venice is a remarkably quiet city, but for light sleepers there is the hazard of church bells in the early morning and the hooters and bellowing diesels of barges on the wider canals. For most visitors the chance of such disturbance is an acceptable risk and everyone benefits from a car-free city.

# Fabrics & Glass

### Opening Hours

Most Italian shops close for a long lunch but they do stay open later in the day; 9–1, 4–8. Most shops close on Sunday; many close for a half day on Monday morning or Wednesday afternoon. However, shops catering for tourists often stay open through the lunch break and on Sundays, in particular during the summer. Food stores often open earlier at 8 or 8.30.

### Material Wealth

As can be seen in the paintings of Venetian life in past centuries, richly coloured and textured fabrics were always favoured. They still are and a new process of printing part-rayon fabric with traditional Venetian designs has produced a new range suitable for curtains, loose covers, cushion covers and bedspreads. The big fashion houses are also buying these sumptuous materials for their latest designs..

Lace has been made and sold by the women of the island of Burano beyond Murano for centuries, but beware; sadly much is now factory-made in the Far East. The traditional work is repetitive and skilled and takes its toll on the women's eyesight and consequently, fewer and fewer Buranese women practise the art.

## Fabrics

### Bevilacqua

This shop has an exquisite selection of both machine and handwoven fabrics, some made on original 17th-century looms. The Italian fashion houses, such as Dolce & Gabanna, come to this shop for the wonderful velvets, taffetas, damasks, satins and brocades. If you can't afford much, the curtain ties and key tassels make gorgeous souvenirs.

**✉ Fondamenta della Canonica, San Marco 337/B ☎ 041 528 7581; www.luigi-bevilacqua.com 🚤 San Zaccaria/Giglio**

### Gaggio

Some of the patterns in this shop are those once favoured by the designer and artist Mariano Fortuny (1871–1949), best remembered for the light, pleated silk dresses he produced. Wonderful hand-printed materials for a plethora of expensive products—cushions, bags, hats, dresses and more.

**✉ Calle delle Botteghe, San Marco 3441–3451 ☎ 041 522 8574; www.gaggio.com 🚤 San Samuele**

### Trois

Mariano Fortuny's fabric designs are the specialty of this shop in San Marco, and it is the only place in Venice where you can buy.his original fabrics and the price is better than in the US or UK. Also stocks small antiques and has a special line in beadwork.

**✉ Campo San Maurizio, San Marco 2666 ☎ 041 522 2905 🚤 Giglio**

## Glass

### Barovier e Toso

A fine exponent of Murano glass and one of the best in Murano. The family has been involved in glass production since the 14th century, owning some 26,000 pieces of antique glass.

**✉ Fondamenta dei Vetrai 28, Murano ☎ 041 739 049 🚤 Murano DM (Colonna/Faro)**

### Mazzega

The best in elegant table glassware can be bought in this shop in Murano. They also give demonstrations of glass sculpture and chandelier production.

**✉ Fondamental da Mula 147, Murano ☎ 041 736 888; 🚤 Murano DM (Museo/Venier)**

### Pauly

Right on the doorstep of San Marco, this is one of the city's best outlets for Murano glass. The emphasis is on modern design, with the use of clean lines and bright colours, although there are some traditional pieces as well, plus some glass jewellery.

**✉ Ponte Consorzi, Calle Larga, San Marco 4391/A ☎ 041 520 9899; www.paulyglassfactory.com 🚤 Vallaresso (San Marco)**

### Rossana e Rossana

Traditional Venetian glass-making combined with contemporary design. High quality produced with superb technique and crafts-manship. Choose from vases, glasses, frames and wonderful replicas of shells, oysters and sea creatures.

**✉ Riva Lunga, Murano 11 ☎ 041 527 4076; www.ro-e-ro.com 🚤 Murano DM (Venier)**

# Jewellery, Leather & Shoes

## Jewellery

**Antichità**
Particularly special here are antique beads, which you can have made up on the spot into individual necklaces. Plus other jewellery, antiques and lace.
**✉ Calle Toletta, Dorsoduro 1195 ☏ 041 522 3159 ⛴ Accademia**

**Anticlea Antiquariato**
One of the best for antique glass beads in the city, the shop is stuffed full with every colour and style. They will make up necklaces, braclets or earrings for you or you can buy ready-made.
**✉ Calle San Provolo, Castello 4719/A ☏ 041 528 6946 ⛴ San Zaccaria**

**Laberintho**
In a tiny street, you will find young designers making up some individual and inspired pieces of jewellery using inlaid stone settings.
**✉ Calle del Scaleter, San Polo 2236 ☏ 041 571 0017 ⛴ San Tomà**

## Leather Goods & Shoes

**Bottega Veneta**
With branches throughout the world, you can see the latest lines here first. Gorgeous soft leathers for bags, belts, wallets and purses. They may be pricey but they last.
**✉ Calle Vallaresso, San Marco 1337 ☏ 041 522 8489 ⛴ Vallresso (San Marco)**

**Calzature Casella**
A Venetian institution and high in quality. Popular with tourists, they continue to bring out classic shoe designs but there will be variations every season, bringing tradition up to date.
**✉ Campo San Salvador, San Marco 5048 ☏ 041 522 8848 ⛴ Rialto**

**Calzoloeria La Parigina**
Located in the Mercerie shopping district, you can find all manner of well-known shoe brands and some lesser known fun styles. Two well-known names include Clarks and Timberland. Look too for John Lobb and Vicini among the lesser known makes. You can find another branch near the Scala di Bolovlo at San Marco 4336.
**✉ Merzaria San Zulian, San Marco 727 ☏ 041 523 1555 ⛴ Vallaresso (San Marco)**

**Furla**
If you're into handbags you will be in heaven here; every hue in funky designs. Other leather accessories, including belts and gloves.
**✉ Mercerie del Capitello, San Marco 4954 ☏ 041 523 0611 ⛴ Rialto**

**Italo Marini**
Frequented by locals, you can get stylish shoes and boots plus some good value bags and briefcases. If you are here in January check out their sale.
**✉ Calle del Teatro, San Marco 4775 ☏ 041 523 5580 ⛴ Rialto**

**Sergio Rossi**
For cutting edge in the latest leather shoes for men and women you should visit this shop. Big range and helpful and friendly staff.
**✉ Mercerie San Zulian, San Marco 705 ☏ 041 241 3615 ⛴ Vallaresso (San Marco)**

**Glass**
Surprisingly, the Venetians, who have always had such good taste in art and architecture, have turned out a remarkable amount of vulgar knick-knacks during their millennium of glass-making. Today the bulk of the glass on display in shop windows and showrooms is over-ornate, impractical, difficult to use and easy to break. That said, it is worth searching for the beautiful pieces that are still made with a purity of design and strong Venetian character.
For eight centuries, Murano has been the glass-making island. Glass shops and showrooms abound in the city itself but for the real thing Murano must be visited. Retailers and manufacturers are efficient at packing and freighting your purchases.

# Crafts, Food & Drink & Markets

### Metalwork

Small foundries and smithies still abound in the alleys of Venice, notably to the north of the Campo San Barnaba. They not only manufacture brass souvenirs—such as Lion of St. Mark paperweights—but make practical and attractive coat hooks, door knockers and so on. Some of the old, established workshops also stock antique metalwork, which is not expensive. There are many silver shops and some silversmiths throughout the city. Most of their stock is manufactured elsewhere—such as the charming little silver boxes fashioned like sea shells—but a few both manufacture and sell.

## Masks

### Balocoloc

Papier-mâche masks as well as carnival costumes can be bought at this shop. It also stocks a remarkable range of hats, all original and handmade by the owner, Silvana Martin, who changes her designs seasonally—from berets to brims.

**✉ Calle Lunga, Santa Croce 2134 ☎ 041 524 0551 ⛴ San Silvestro**

### Mondo Novo

There are so many mask shops in Venice, so how do you know which one to choose? Try this little gem, which is one of the most famous in the city and has been making masks for years. It's good because it combines the traditional with the modern and the workmanship is highly skilled, producing a beautiful end product.

**✉ Ria Terrà Canal, Dorsoduro 3063 ☎ 041 528 7344 ⛴ Ca' Rezzonico**

### Tragicomica

All the fun of the fair—masks and costumes for the carnival can be brought from Tragicomica. Here you can gain an insight into the origins of the Carnevale; all the 18th-century characters are represented through fantastic craftsmanship.

**✉ Calle dei Nomboli, San Polo 2800 ☎ 041 721 102 ⛴ San Tomà**

## Paper & Stationery

### Ebrû

A particularly elegant stock of hand-printed paper and silk is offered by Alberto Valese-Ebru, who was at the forefront of the revival in Venetian marbled paper in the 1970s. Gorgeous gifts to take home—notebooks, frames, boxes and, of course, paper in a range of delectable hues.

**✉ Campiello Santo Stefano, San Marco 3471 ☎ 041 523 8830 ⛴ Accademia**

### Legatoria Piazzesi

In business since 1900, this is one of the last workshops in the city to use the traditional wood-block method of printing to hand print beautiful marbled paper, books and stationery. It's expensive but it is stunning and you can always buy a single sheet to take home as a souvenir.

**✉ Campiello della Fettrina, San Marco 2511 ☎ 041 522 1202 ⛴ Giglio**

### Paolo Olbi

Signor Olbi was another craftsman involved in the revival of marbled paper and the selection at his shop is wonderful. Come here for that special gift.

**✉ Calle della Mandola, San Marco 3653 ☎ 041 528 5025 ⛴ Sant'Angelo**

## Woodwork

### Gianni Cavalier

Venetian craftsman producing painted and gilded furniture and frames for both pictures and mirrors—which make cheaper and more portable gifts. He still uses the centuries old baroque designs and traditional gilding methods.

**✉ Campo San Stefano, San Marco 2863/A ☎ 041 523 8621 ⛴ Accademia**

**Gilbert Penzo**
World-renowned maker of replica wooden gondolas. Superb craftsman, Penzo turns his hands to other Venetian boats as well. If you can't afford the real thing, you can buy kits to make your own when you get home.
**✉ Calle Seconda dei Saoneri, San Polo 2681 ☎ 041 719 372 🚢 San Tomà**

**Livio de Marchi**
It's not everyday you see ordinary objects so beautifully carved in wood—a coat on a hanger, a pair of socks, a handbag or a hat. They are expensive but they are magnificent and the shop is definitely worth a good browse.
**✉ Salizzada San Samuele, San Marco 3157/A ☎ 041 528 5694; www.liviodemarchi.com 🚢 San Samuele**

**Spazio Legno**
One of the most unusual gifts you could buy, made by Saverior Pastor, a master *marangon* (oar maker), is his specialty, the elaborately carved *forcole*, the gondola rowlock (oarlock). Crafted in walnut, each is unique and originally only made for the gondolier; now they are works of art in their own right.
**✉ Fondamenta San Giacomo, Guidecca 213/B ☎ 041 277 5505 🚢 Redentore**

## Food & Drink

**Casa del Parmigia**
It may be small but this is said to be one of the best delis in Venice. The selection of cheeses from all over Italy is as superb as it is mouth-watering. Homemade pastas, salamis, wines and olive oils—great for gifts.
**✉ Erberia Rilaton, San Polo 214/215 ☎ 041 520 6525 🚢 Sant'Angelo**

**Drogheria Mascari**
A family business since 1948, this lovely shop is brimming with all manner of treats. A wondrous collection of wines, liquors, spices, teas and special sweets and much much more. Superb.
**✉ Ruga Spezieri, San Polo 381 ☎ 041 022 9762 🚢 Rialto**

**Vinaira Nave de Oro**
One of several branches in the city that will fill up your plastic water bottles from a selection of wines. Very helpful staff give direction.
**✉ Campo Santa Marherita, Dorsoduro 3664 ☎ 041 522 2693 🚢 Ca' Rezzonico**

## Markets

**Pescherie**
Not for the weak-stomached but an experience nevertheless. This fish market, by the Grand Canal, is worth a look for its squid, crabs and strange-looking fish.
**✉ Fondamenta dell'Olio, San Polo 🕐 Tue–Sat 8–1 🚢 Rialto**

**Rialto**
A 1,000-year-old trading station and although most produce is shipped from the mainland, it's good stuff.
**✉ Ruga dei Orefici, San Polo 🕐 Mon–Sat 8–1 🚢 Rialto**

**Via Garibaldi**
So different from the rest of Venice, this wide street is host to a great produce market. Lots of local life.
**✉ Via Guiseppe Garibaldi, Castello 🕐 Mon–Sat 8–1 🚢 Arsenale**

**More Markets**
Stalls selling silk scarves and ties and leather goods are set up at either end of the Rialto Bridge, upon which are two parallel rows of little shops selling jewellery, leather goods, silks and shoes. Stalls are also found in the Strada Nuova and those selling souvenirs congregate along the Riva degli Schiavoni; these include artists' mass-producing views of Venice and offering instant caricatures. About twice a year an antiques market is held in the Campo San Maurizio.

# Fashion

**Designer City**
Did you think that Italian fashion was synononous with Milan, or maybe Rome? Surprisingly Venice has a plethora of smart clothes shops that the fashion-conscious can spend a day window-shopping instead of looking at old master paintings or historic churches. All the top designer names are here and you will find them in the San Marco district. Check out Emporio Armani, Fendi, Fratelli Rossetti, Gucci, Max Mara, Missoni, Prado, Valentino and of course Versace.

## For Men

### Al Duca di Aosta
Beloved by Italian men, this is the place to come for classic, smart clothes but with a dash of modernity. International labels such as Burberry and the latest styles from the likes of Burini, Kiton and Fay.
**✉ Mercerie, San Marco 4922–4926 ☎ 041 522 0733 ⛴ Rialto**

### Camicieria San Marco
Shirts and more shirts. Everything from top-brands to made to measure is here. Plus ties, pyjamas and bathrobes.
**✉ Calle Vallaresso, San Marco 1340 ☎ 041 522 1432 ⛴ Vallaresso (San Marco)**

### Paul and Shark
A big name in men's casual wear, this is the place to come for well-tailored, comfortable clothes and sportswear. Choose from smart casual to relaxed.
**✉ Mercerie, San Marco 4844 ☎ 041 523 7733 ⛴ Rialto**

## For Women

### Agnona
The ultimate classics in natural fibres—wool, linen, silk and cotton. Coolest of colours at a price.
**✉ Calle Vallaresso, San Marco 1316 ☎ 041 522 1432 ⛴ Vallaresso (San Marco)**

### Coin
Probably the most popular, and certainly one of the best, of Italy's chain department stores. A full wardrobe, plus accessories, available at good prices and you can also buy linen and homewares.
**✉ Salizzada San Grisitomo, Cannaregio 5787 ☎ 041 522 1432 ⛴ Rialto**

### Diesel
Well-known throughout Europe, it's worth having a look here, its home base, as the cutting-edge clothing is less expensive than you will find elsewhere.
**✉ Calle dei Fabbri, San Marco 4664 ☎ 041 241 1937 ⛴ Rialto**

### Emporio Armani
As in every Italian city this well-known fashion house is a good place to start exploring the chicest of clothes on offer.
**✉ Calle dei Fabbri, San Marco 989 ☎ 041 523 7808 ⛴ Rialto**

### La Fenice Atelier
Beautiful lingerie and night-wear in superior materials. Exquisite table linens, too.
**✉ Calle dei Frati, San Marco 3537 ☎ 041 523 0578 ⛴ Sant'Angelo**

### Laura Biagiotta
Big name in Italian fashion, these clothes are for today's woman whose wardrobe features urban items with natural touches. Tradition and modernity combine for an up-to-the-minute image.
**✉ Calle Larga (Viale) XXII Marzo, San Marco 2400/A ☎ 041 520 3401 ⛴ Vallresso (San Marco)**

### Mistero
Three shops next door to each other: young fashion, ladies' clothes (including larger sizes) and homeware. Atelier, selling the women's clothes, has some lovely items imported from India.
**✉ Ruga Giuffa, Castello 4755 ☎ 041 522 7797 ⛴ San Zaccaria**

# For Children

**Boat trips**
There's plenty to see on a vaparetto ride along the Grand Canal or out to one of the islands. Arriving by boat from the airport is an exciting experience.

**Watching the pigeons**
Love them or hate them, you can't avoid these birds in San Marco. It's best not to feed them as they can be a nuisance. Just have a look.

**Glass-blowing**
Watching the glassblowers at work, even at one of the demonstration furnaces in the city, is enthralling and children need no persuading to start collecting little—and inexpensive—glass animals.

**Gondolas**
It does cost a lot, but it's by the boat, not by the person, so a family of up to five can be accommodated.

**Ice Cream**
Every flavour under the sun. Treat the kids at one of the city's best *gelatarie*—try Paolin (► 98) or Nico (► 97).

**Islands**
Take a trip to Murano to see the glassblowing, Burano for the pretty houses or Torcello for a walk. Don't forget the smaller islands either; try Sant'Erasmo, where you can walk, cycle, take a picnic or head for the little beach.

**Lido**
The Lido offers a chance to swim or play on the beach. You can rent bicycles or pedaloes from outlets on the front. Look for the public beaches; many are owned by hotels and are private.

**Masks**
They're everywhere and the variety is fascinating, from creepy faces to animal heads.

**Museums**
For would-be historians try the following: the Museo Storico Navale (► 45), with its beautifully constructed model ships and the displays of the glories of Venice's maritime past; the Palazzo Ducale (► 20), where you'll need to be brave to venture into the palace's dungeons with the spine-tingling torture chambers.

**Parks and Playgrounds**
The best park in Venice, with a few swings and slides, is the surprisingly spacious Giardini Pubblici in Castello. You can walk along the waterfront or take a picnic.

**Puntalaguna**
Plenty of interactives here in this multimedia centre devoted to ecology and the state of the lagoon. Runs workshops for children (► 50).

**Swimming**
A new pool (Piscina Comunale Sant' Alvise ✉ Calle del Capitello, Cannaregio 3163 ☎ 041 713 567) offers swimming sessions and lessons as well as a mini-pool for little kids. You have to wear a swimming hat in the water and flip flops from the changing rooms to the water.

**Towers**
Get a bird's-eye view of Venice from the top of the Campanile in Piazza San Marco or the church on the island of San Giorgio Maggiore.

**Football (soccer)**
Stadio Penzo is the only league ground in Europe to be entirely surrounded by water. It is located on the island of Sant'Elena in eastern Castello. The local team, A.C. Venezia, is in the Serie B league, having risen temporarily to Serie A from 1998 to 2000. The season runs from September until June, with the team playing on alternate Saturdays and Sundays. The opposing team arrives by train and is then transferred by boat to the island. You can get tickets at the stadium and at ACTV and VeLa offices. (For more information check the website www.veneziacalcio.it).

# Theatre, Dance, Opera & Ballet

### What's On

There are several newspapers and magazines that will give information about films, concerts and exhibitions in Venice. Look for the *Spettacoli* section of the daily newspapers such as *Il Gazzettino* and *La Nuova Venzia.* Another good source is the free Italian/English magazine *Un Ospite di Venezia* ( a Guest in Venice; www.aguestinvenice.com) available from tourist offices and many hotels. It is published weekly in high season, monthly low season. There are always plenty of posters around advertising forthcoming events. Tickets are ususally available directly from the venue concerned and there are a few travel agencies where you can buy tickets. For some events tickets are available from VeLa outlets in the city (part of the transport group ACTV).

## Theatre

### Teatrino Groggia

This is a bit far out but this intimate little theatre is praised for its modern and contemporary productions and concerts. It is a showcase for aspiring Italian writers, but it does put on the occasional production in English. Concerts range from traditional American folk to minimalist contemporary.

**✉ Calle del Capitello, Cannaregio 3161 ☎ 041 524 4665 ⛴ Sant'Alvise**

### Teatro da l'Avogaria

Founded in 1969 by the late, internationally renowned director Giovanni Poli, this theatre specializes in experimental drama. It stages works by little-known playwrights from the 15th to 19th centuries.

**✉ Corte Zappa, Dorsoduro 1617 ☎ 041 520 6130 ⛴ San Basilio**

### Teatro Carlo Goldoni

Venice's principal venue for Italian and international drama, mostly performed in Italian, is named after Venice's greatest playwright. Also hosts some pop concerts usually featuring Italian artists.

**✉ Calle Goldini, San Marco 4650/B ☎ 041 240 2011 ⛴ Rialto**

## Contemporary Dance

### Teatro Fondamente Nuove

Located in an old carpenter's shop, this is Venice's foremost avant-garde venue. Works staged include contemporary dance, workshops and exhibitions as well as film festivals and innovative arts projects.

**✉ Fondamente Nuove, Cannaregio 5013 ☎ 041 522 4498 ⛴ Fondamente Nuove**

### Teatro Verde

A great setting in parkland, this open-air theatre on the island of San Giorgio was founded in 1954 and renovated in the late 1990s. Belonging to the Fondazione Cine, it mainly stages contemporary dance during the summer.

**✉ Isola di San Giorgio Maggiore ☎ 041 528 990 ⛴ San Giorgio**

## Opera & Ballet

### Teatrino Malibran

This was the city's original theatre, playing a central role in cultural life since it was founded in 1678. It had fallen into disrepair by the 1970s but underwent restoration and reopened in 2001 and staged La Fenice productions. It produces well-known operas, modern works, ballet and classical concerts.

**✉ Calle dei Milion, Cannaregio 5873 ☎ 041 786 603; box office 041 899 909 090 ⛴ Rialto**

### Teatro La Fenice

After many years of restoration following the disastrous fire of 1996, La Fenice (► 68) has finally re-opened and it is worth visiting just for the magnificent building itself. It is primarily an opera house but also stages ballet and concerts. Reservations for tickets are essential; obtain in advance from the box office, by telephone or on internet.

**✉ Campo San Fantin, San Marco 1965; www.teatroafenice.it ☎ 041 240 2011 ⛴ Giglio**

# Classical Music & Cinema

## Classical Music

**Basilica dei Frari**
A good mix of religious music, orchestral pieces and organ recitals.
**✉ Campo dei Frari, San Polo ☎ 041 522 2637 ⛴ San Tomà**

**Chiesa di San Giacometto**
Said to be the oldest church in Venice, it plays host to the Ensemble Antonio Vivaldi who presents concerts in this wonderful interior.
**✉ Campo di San Giacometto, San Polo ☎ 041 426 6559; www.prgroup.it ⛴ San Silvestro**

**Fondazione Querini Stampalia**
Regular Friday and Saturday concerts in this elegant 15th-century palazzo.
**✉ Campo Querini Stampalia, Castell 5252 ☎ 041 271 1411; www.querinistampalia.it ⛴ San Zaccaria**

**La Pietà (Santa Maria della Visitazione)**
Vivaldi worshipped here and was the Master of Concerts. Today his work is celebrated along with other well-known composers, including Handel.
**✉ Riva degli Schiavoni, San Marco ☎ 041 523 1096; www.vivaldi.it ⛴ San Zaccaria**

**Santa Maria della Salute**
A wonderful venue to listen to organ music. Listen during Sunday Mass at 11am to the resident organist or to visiting guest performers.
**✉ Campo della Salute, Dorsoduro ☎ 041 522 5558 ⛴ Salute**

**Scoula Grande di San Rocco**
With a musical tradition stretching back over 500 years, this is a superb setting to hear baroque music such as that by Monteverdi.
**✉ Campo San Rocco ☎ 041 523 4864 ⛴ San Tomà**

**Scoula Grande di San Teodoro**
A superb venue for the baroque and operatic concerts that are held from May to November.
**✉ Salizzada San Teodoro, San Marco 4810 ☎ 041 521 0294 ⛴ Rialto**

## Cinemas

**Arena di Campo Polo**
From late July to early September the square is transformed into an open-air cinema.
**✉ Campo San Polo, San Polo ☎ 041 524 1320 ⛴ San Silvestro**

**Girogione Movie D'Essai**
Screens art-house films and mainstreams that are dubbed into Italian. There are English versions on Tuesdays from October to May; also children's films on weekends.
**✉ Rio Terrà dei Franceschi, Cannaregio 4612 ☎ 041 522 6298 ⛴ Ca' d'Oro**

**Palazzo del Cinema**
Home to Venice's Film Festival (► 116). Tickets go quickly for the premieres. Also hosts fashion shows.
**✉ Lungomre Marconi, Lido 90 ☎ 041 521 8711; www.labiennale.com ⛴ Lido 1**

**Videoteca Pasinetti**
Primarily a resource and archive centre with a vast collection of Venice-related film; it also shows movies, videos and newsreels.
**✉ Palazzo Carminati, Salizzada Carminati, Santa Croce 1882 ☎ 041 524 1320 ⛴ San Stae**

**Music in the City**
Venice has always been steeped in music from classical and religious to crooning gondoliers. It has some of the most evocative venues in Italy, and its association with Vivaldi puts it firmly in the frame for some of the best baroque music around.
The city has several resident ochestras, including the Orchestra di Venezia; I Musici Venezia (resplendent in 18th-century costume), and the Concerti della Venzia Musica who are especially devoted to the work of Vivaldi.
It is rare to see contemporary bands play in Venice, the nearest likely venue being on the mainland at Mestre. For live music on a small scale—jazz, blues or pop—you will need to check out a handful of bars or restaurants that occasionally offer such music (► 114–115).

# Bars, Clubs & Casinos

**Early to Bed**
Venice goes to bed—or at least home—early and not long after 10pm the alleys become quiet. However, there are areas that keep going longer and where it is easy enough to get a drink. Particularly vibrant as the evening wears on is Campo Santa Margherita in the student district of Dorsoduro.

## Bars

### Bacaro Jazz
A great welcome from the host, a Cuban and excellent cocktail mixer. Jazz and locals (expect some gondoliers) means a lively night. Good food, too.
**Salizzida del Fontego dei Tedeschi, San Marco 041 528 5249 Daily Thu–Tue 11am–2am Giglio**

### Café dei Frari
Popular with students from the university, this is a great place for an aperitif before getting a meal nearby.
**Fondamenta dei Frari, San Polo 2564 041 524 1877 Mon–Sat 9am–9am San Tomà**

### Green Pub
Not everyone's cup of tea or pint of beer but it is located in the heart of Venice's nightlife and is popular. A bit of Britain in town.
**Campo Santa Margherita, Dorsoduro 3053/A 041 520 5976 Fri–Wed 7.30am–2am Ca' Rezzonico**

### Haig's Bar
Close to the Gritti Palace Hotel (► 102), this bar, an American-style piano bar, stays open late.
**Campo del Giglio, San Marco 2477 041 528 9456 Daily 1.30–3, 7–2 Giglio**

### Harry's Bar
This celebrated bar's (► 96) specialty is the Bellini—peach juice and champagne. The house wines are also excellent.
**Calle Vallaresso, San Marco 1323 041 528 577 Daily 9.30am–11pm Vallaresso (San Marco)**

### Iguana
If sangria, burritos, fajitas and singing is your thing, this Mexican bar is just the place to let your hair down.
**Fondmenta della Misericordia, Canneregio 2515 041 713 561 Tue–Sun 8am–2am Madonna dell'Orto**

### Il Caffè
Another popular haunt that stays open later than most and is located in a lovely square. Popular for coffee by day, it becomes the focal point of the campo at night.
**Campo Santa Margherita, Dorsoduro 2963 041 528 7998 Mon–Sat 7.30am–2am Ca' Rezzonico**

### Inishark
Okay so it's another Irish pub abroad but it's a nice one and you get a very warm welcome from the Italian owners. Guinness to drink and football (soccer) on the wide-screen TV.
**Calle del Mondo Novo, Castello 5787 041 717 999 Daily 5pm–1am Rialto**

### La Cantina
There are lots of bars in the Strada Nuova area but this one is probably the best. Beers on tap and good wines; it's just nice to drop into.
**Campo San Felice, Cannaregio 3689 041 522 8258 Mon–Sat 9–8.30 Ca' d'Oro**

### Margaret Duchamp
This is one of the liveliest areas in the city, and you can get a good choice of beer here plus a reasonable selection of wines.
**Campo Santa Margherita, Dorsoduro 3019 041 528 6255 Daily 9am–2am San Tomà**

**Vino Vino**
Lovely place to enjoy a glass of wine (this is not the place for beer) in a bar that also serves food. Diverse crowd.
**Calle delle Veste, San Marco 2007/A 041 241 688 Wed–Mon 10.30am–midnight Vallaresso (San Marco)**

**Vitae**
A designer bar aimed at the upwardly mobile. Choose from beers, *spritz* or cocktails. Lively.
**Calle Sant' Antonio, San Marco 4118 041 520 5205 Mon–Sat 9pm–1am Rialto**

## Clubs

**Casanova**
Up near the train station, this internet café doubles up as a club and attracts a mixed bunch—tourists, students and the gay and lesbian crowd. It is probably the city's only true nightclub.
**Lista di Spagna, Cannaregio 158/A 041 275 0199 Wed–Sat 6pm–3am Ferrovia**

**Floridita**
Away from the tourist trail, this area is where the locals hang out. You can't get out of dancing here to the beat of salsa and merengue.
**Via Guiseppe Garibaldi, Castello 68 041 419 6963 Fri 9pm–4am Arsenale**

**Piccolo Mondo**
Decorated in retro 1970s style, this tiny bar/club is popular with students and a well-dressed thirty-something Italian crowd.
**Calle Contarini Corfù, Dorsoduro 1056 041 520 0371 Daily 9pm–4am Accademia**

**Round Midnight**
House, acid jazz and Latin feature at this small club around the corner from Campo San Margherita. You have to look carefully for it as it looks like a residential house. Pricey drinks but the next best thing to a club outside Venice.
**Calle dei Pugli, Fondamenta di Squero, Dorsoduro 3102 041 523 2056 Mon–Sat 9pm–2am Ca' Rezzonico**

## Casinos

**Casinò Municipale**
On the Canal Grande in the opulent Palazzo Vendramin-Calergi, the Casinó offers roulette, baccarat and blackjack, as well as slot machines and electronic games. You will have to be smart—dress code is jacket and tie for men.
**Palazzo Vendramin Calergi, Calle Largo Vendramin, of Rio Terrà della Maddalena, Cannaregio 2040 041 529 7111; www.casinovenezia.it Daily 2.45pm–2.30am (slot machines daily 11am–3am) San Marcuola**

**Venice Casino Ca' Noghera**
Busy, flashy and popular, this informal modern casino opened in 2001 near Mestre on the mainland. Run by the same company as the Casinò Municipale (► above), it offers a similar range of table games and slot machines.
**Ca' Noghera, Via Triestina, Tessera 222 041 529 7111; www.casinovenezia.it Sun–Fri 4pm–3.45am, Sat 4pm–4.45am (slot machines Sun–Fri 11am–4.45am, Sat 11am–6am) Free hourly shuttle from Piazzale Roma**

**No Place for Clubbing**
The club scene is virtually non-existent in Venice and apart from the few on this page you will need to go to the mainland—the closest is Mestre—if you want to dance the night away. There is a bit more choice in the summer over on the Lido, but the main action takes place along the coast at the resort of Lido di Jésolo (► 85).

# What's On When

### Island Festivities

On the 15th August each year Venetians head for the island of Torcello for a holiday weekend of activities and concerts to celebrate *Ferragosto* (the Assumption of the Virgin). On the third Sunday in September Burano plays hosts to a fish festival, *Sagre del Pesce*, when a good deal of fried fish is eaten and much white wine consumed. It is followed by the last regatta of the season. The first weekend of October is the time for the festival *Sagra del Mosta* (grape juice festival) on the farming island of Sant' Erasmo. With the festival dedicated to the grape harvest, much jollity ensues, with sideshows, food stands and, of course, much consumption of the local juice.

**January**
*Regata della Befana* (6 Jan): The first of more than 100 regattas to be held on the lagoon throughout the year is on Epiphany.

**February**
*Carnevale* (10 days before Lent): The carnival was abolished by the French in 1797 but revived in 1979 with great success. At first largely a Venetian festival, it is now international and, some complain, over-elaborate. Masks and fancy dress—which can be bought or hired in the city—are worn all day and most of the night. A daily schedule of events includes dancing at night in a campo, where mulled wine and traditional sugared cakes are sold from stands.

**April**
*Festa di San Marco* (25 Apr): The feast day of St. Mark, Venice's patron saint. A gondola race from Sant'Elena to the Punta della Dogna marks the day and men give women a red rose.

**May**
*Festa della Sensa* (Sunday after Ascencion Day): the Mayor of Venice re-enacts the ceremony of the Marriage of Venice with the Sea. In the old days, the Doge would be rowed out to sea in his ceremonial barge to cast a gold wedding ring into the Adriatic, but the occasion is now only a faint echo of the original.
*Vogalonga* (Sunday following *La Sensa*): a 32km (20-mile) rowing race in which anyone can join in any type of oared boat from San Marco to Burano and back.

**June**
Every odd-numbered year (Jun–end Sep): International arts exhibition.
*Festa di San Pietro* (last weekend in Jun): Celebrates the feast of St. Peter centred on his church in Castello, a lively event with concerts, dancing and food stands.

**July**
*Festa del Redentore* (third weekend in Jul): Involves the building of a bridge of boats across the Giudecca Canal to the church of the Redentore and was begun as a festival in thanksgiving for the ending of a plague more than four centuries ago. Picnics and fireworks.

**August/September**
*Mostra del Cinema Venezia* (12 days from last week in Aug): The high-profile international Venice Film Festival is held on the Lido; it's Italy's version of Cannes.

**September**
*Regata Storica* (first Sunday in Sep): The most spectacular event of the Venetian year, it involves gondola races and a procession up the Grand Canal of boats and barges manned by Venetians in historic costume.

**November**
*Festa della Salute* (21 Nov): A procession makes its way across the Grand Canal on floating bridges to the church of the Salute to give thanks for the ending of another plague of 1630.

**December**
*La Befana* (Christmas, New Year): Celebrations for the festive season.

# Practical Matters

Above: *A vaparetto plies the Grand Canal near San Marco*
Right: *A silver and gold sun and moon emblem on a shop in Venice*

## TIME DIFFERENCES

|  |  |  |  |  |  |
|---|---|---|---|---|---|
| | → | → | ← | → | → |
| GMT 12 noon | Italy 1pm | Germany 1pm | USA (NY) 7am | Netherlands 1pm | Spain 1pm |

# BEFORE YOU GO

## WHAT YOU NEED

● Required
○ Suggested
▲ Not required

Some countries require a passport to remain valid for a minimum period (usually at least six months) beyond the date of entry—contact their consulate or embassy or your travel agent for details.

| | UK | Germany | USA | Netherlands | Spain |
|---|---|---|---|---|---|
| Passport or National Identity Card where applicable | ● | ● | ● | ● | ● |
| Visa (regulations can change—check before booking your journey) | ▲ | ▲ | ▲ | ▲ | ▲ |
| Onward or return ticket | ▲ | ▲ | ▲ | ▲ | ▲ |
| Health inoculations | ▲ | ▲ | ▲ | ▲ | ▲ |
| Health documentation (➤ 123, Health) | ● | ● | ● | ● | ● |
| Travel insurance | ○ | ○ | ○ | ○ | ○ |
| Driving licence (national with Italian translation or international) | ● | ● | ● | ● | ● |
| Car insurance certificate (if own car) | ● | ● | ● | ● | ● |
| Car registration document (if own car) | ● | ● | ● | ● | ● |

## WHEN TO GO

**Venice**

High season (APR–SEP)
Low season (JAN–MAR, OCT–DEC)

| JAN | FEB | MAR | APR | MAY | JUN | JUL | AUG | SEP | OCT | NOV | DEC |
|---|---|---|---|---|---|---|---|---|---|---|---|
| 6°C | 8°C | 12°C | 15°C | 20°C | 23°C | 26°C | 25°C | 21°C | 16°C | 12°C | 7°C |
| Cloud | Cloud | Wet | Sunshine/Showers | Sunshine/Showers | Sunshine/Showers | Sun | Sun | Sun | Sunshine/Showers | Wet | Cloud |

 Wet   Cloud  Sun  Sunshine/ Showers

## TOURIST OFFICES

**In the UK**
Italian State Tourist Office (ENIT)
1 Princes Street
London W1B 2AY
☎ 020 7493 6695
Fax 020 7399 3567

**In the US**
Italian State Tourist Office (ENIT)
630 Fifth Avenue
Suite 1565
New York
☎ (212) 245 4822

NATIONAL POLICE (Polizia di Stato) 113

CITY POLICE (Carabinieri) 112

FIRE (Vigili del Fuoco) 115

AMBULANCE (Ambulància) 118

## WHEN YOU ARE THERE

### ARRIVING

There are direct flights to Venice from all over the world. Scheduled flights arrive at Venice's Marco Polo airport, while the city's second airport, Treviso, caters mostly for charter flights. Trains to Venice arrive at Venezia Santa Lucia station, located at the head of the

**Marco Polo Airport**
Distance to city centre

13km (8 miles)

| **Journey times** | |
|---|---|
| Boat | 50 minutes |
| Bus | 25 minutes |
| Car | 15 minutes |

**Treviso Airport**
Distance to city centre

30km (19 miles)

| **Journey times** | |
|---|---|
| Train | N/A |
| Bus | 45 minutes |
| Car | 35 minutes |

### MONEY

The euro (€) is the official currency of Italy. Euro banknotes and coins were introduced in January 2002. Banknotes are issued in denominations of 5, 10, 20, 50, 100, 200 and 500 euros; coins in denominations of 1, 2, 5, 10, 20 and 50 cents, and 1 and 2 euros.

### TIME

Venice is one hour ahead of Greenwich Mean Time (GMT + 1), but from late March, when clocks are put forward one hour, until late October, Italian summer time (GMT + 2) operates.

### CUSTOMS

**YES**

**Goods obtained Duty Free inside the EU or goods bought outside the EU (Limits):**
Alcohol (over 22% vol): 1L or
Alcohol (not over 22% vol): 2L
*and*
Still table wine: 2L,
Cigarettes: 200 *or* Cigars: 50
*or* Tobacco: 250gm
Perfume: 60ml
Toilet water: 250ml
**Goods bought Duty and Tax Paid for own use inside the EU (Guidance Levels):**
Alcohol (over 22% vol): 10L
Alcohol (not over 22% vol): 20L *and* Wine (max 60L sparkling): 90L Beer: 110L
Cigarettes: 800, Cigars: 200, Tobacco: 1kg
Perfume and Toilet Water: no limit
**You must be 17 or over to benefit from alcohol and tobacco allowances.**

**NO**

Drugs, firearms, ammunition, offensive weapons, obscene material, unlicensed animals.

## CONSULATES

|  |  |  |  |  |
|---|---|---|---|---|
| USA in Milan 02 290351 | UK 041 5227207 | Germany 041 5237675 | Netherlands 041 5283416 | Spain 041 5203709 |

# WHEN YOU ARE THERE

## TOURIST OFFICES

**Head Office**

- Palazetto del Selva Giardinetti Reale San Marco ☎ 041 529 8711; www.turismovenezia.it

**Branches**

- International Arrivals Hall (airport office) Marco Polo airport ☎ 041 541 5887
- Ferrovia Santa Lucia (train station office) ☎ 041 529 8727
- Piazza San Marco 71 ☎ 041 529 8711
- Piazzale Roma ☎ 041 529 8711
- Gran Viale Santa Maria Elisabetta 6 (Lido office) ☎ 041 541 5721

## NATIONAL HOLIDAYS

| J | F | M | A | M | J | J | A | S | O | N | D |
|---|---|---|---|---|---|---|---|---|---|---|---|
| 2 | | (1) | (2) | 1 | | | 1 | | | 1 | 3 |

| | |
|---|---|
| 1 Jan | New Year's Day |
| 6 Jan | Epiphany |
| Mar/Apr | Easter Monday |
| 25 Apr | Liberation Day and patron saint's day (San Marco) |
| 1 May | Labour Day |
| 15 Aug | Assumption of the Virgin |
| 1 Nov | All Saints' Day |
| 8 Dec | Feast of the Immaculate Conception |
| 25 Dec | Christmas Day |
| 26 Dec | Santo Stefano |

## OPENING HOURS

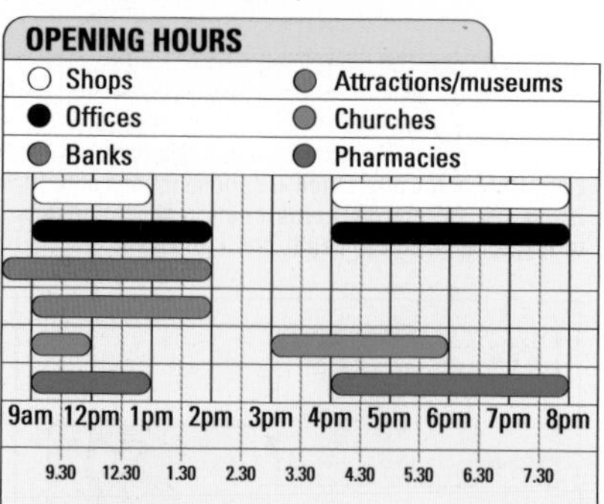


Some tourist shops and supermarkets may also open outside the times shown above, especially in summer. Most food shops close on Wednesday afternoons, while many other shops close Monday mornings (except in summer), and may close Saturday afternoon. Most shops are closed on Sundays.

Some churches are permanently closed except during services; state-run museums usually close Mondays and some museums, such as the Correr, Palazzo Ducale and Guggenheim, stay open all day.

## PUBLIC TRANSPORT

**Vaporetto** The *vaperetto*, or water bus, is operated by the public transport system, ACTV. The main routes run every 10 to 20 minutes during the day. Services are reduced in the evening, especially after midnight. Fast *diretto* boats are more expensive than those that stop at every landing stage. You can buy a ticket for each journey at a ticket office on the pier (if there is one) or pay more for a ticket on board, but if you intend to make six or more journeys in a day, buy a *biglietto giornaliero (*24-hour ticket). If you plan 10 or more journeys within three days buy a *biglietto ore* (72-hour) or a *blochetta* of 10 or more tickets to be used over any period. All tickets must be date-stamped by the automatic machine on the pier before boarding. If you are staying a week, you can buy a weekly *abbonamento* from ticket offices.

**Gondola** A gondola is undoubtedly the most enjoyable means of transport in the city, but also the most expensive—around €80 for four passengers. Fares are governed by a tariff for a 50-minute trip, with a surcharge for night trips after 8pm, but, as gondoliers are notorious for overcharging, it is often easiest to establish terms by ordering a gondola via your tour representative or hotel staff. For a memorable outing, take a two-hour gondola ride down the Grand Canal with a picnic supper on board. Alternatively, consider a cruise operated during the summer months by flotillas of gondolas packed with tourists and entertained by singers—providing an ideal opportunity to explore the waterways at an affordable price.

***Traghetto*** Ferry gondolas—*traghetti*—cross the Grand Canal between special piers at seven different points, providing a vital service for pedestrians. They are indicated by a yellow street sign, illustrated with a tiny gondola symbol. The very reasonable fare (as little as €0.40) is paid to the gondolier on embarkation.

## CAR RENTAL

The leading international car rental companies have offices at Marco Polo airport. Book a car in advance (essential in peak season) either direct or through a travel agent. Bear in mind that driving in the centre of Venice itself is not possible.

## TAXIS

Water-taxis can be hired from 16 water-taxi ranks, including ones at the airport, the railway station, Piazzale Roma, San Marco and the Lido. They can also be ordered by telephone (tel: 041 522 2303). Fares are regulated by a tariff.

## DRIVING

Speed limit on motorways *(autostrade)* **130kph (80mph)**

Speed limit on main roads: **110kph (68mph)**

Speed limit on secondary roads: **90kph (56mph)**

Speed limit in towns: **50kph (31mph)**

Seat belts must be worn in front seats at all times and in rear seats where fitted.

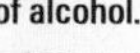

Random breath-testing. Never drive under the influence of alcohol.

Fuel (*benzina)* is more expensive than in the US and most European countries. Filling stations all sell unleaded petrol *(senza piombo)*, but do not always accept credit cards. They are generally open Monday to Saturday 7–12.30 and 3–7.30. Motorway service stations open 24 hours.

In the event of a breakdown ring the Automobile Club d'Italia on 116, giving your location, registration number and type of car, and the nearest ACI office will tow you to the nearest ACI garage. This service is free to foreign vehicles, but you will need to produce your car documentation and passport.

0 1 2 3 4 5 6 7 8
CENTIMETRES

INCHES
0 1 2 3

## PERSONAL SAFETY

To help prevent crime:
- Do not carry more cash around with you than you need
- Beware of pickpockets in markets, tourist sights or crowded places

The main police station, at Via San Nicoladi 22, Marghera (☎ 041 271 5772/041 271 5586) has a special department to deal with visitors' problems

**Police assistance:**
**☎ 112 or 113**

## TELEPHONES

Public telephones take coins, tokens *(gettone)* or phone cards *(schede telfoniche)* which can be bought from SIP offices (the state telephone company) or *tabacchi*, bars and newsstands. You have to break off the marked corner of the phonecard before use.

**International Dialling Codes**
from Venice to:

| | |
|---|---|
| **UK:** | **00 44** |
| **Germany:** | **00 49** |
| **USA:** | **00 1** |
| **Netherlands:** | **00 31** |
| **Spain** | **00 34** |

## POST

Most post offices open Monday to Friday from 8am to 2pm. Some also open on Saturday morning. The main post office *(ufficio postale)* at Palazzo delle Poste (near the Rialto Bridge) is open Monday to Friday 8.15–5.30, and Saturday 8.15–1. You can also buy stamps *(francobolli)* at tobacconists.

## ELECTRICITY

The power supply is 220 volts, but is suitable for 240-volt appliances.

Sockets accept two-round-pin Continental-style plugs.
US visitors should bring a voltage transformer.

## TIPS/GRATUITIES

Yes ✓ No ✕

| | | |
|---|---|---|
| Restaurants (if service not included) | ✓ | 10–15% |
| Cafés/bars (if service not included) | ✓ | €1 min |
| Tour guides | ✓ | €1 min |
| Hairdressers | ✓ | €2 |
| Water-taxis | ✓ | 10% |
| Chambermaids | ✓ | €2 |
| Porters | ✕ | €1 |
| Theatre/cinema usherettes | ✓ | change |
| Cloakroom attendants | ✓ | €1 |
| Toilets | ✓ | 50c min |

## PHOTOGRAPHY

**What to photograph:** the Grand Canal, St Mark's Square, Doge's Palace, hidden alleys and waterways, reflections on the canals and the colourful houses on Burano.
**Best time to photograph:** early morning or late evening, when the light is at its best.
**Where to buy film:** film and camera batteries are readily available from specialist shops and some tourist shops.

## HEALTH

### Insurance

Nationals of EU and certain other countries can get reduced-cost emergency healthcare in Italy with the relevant documentation, although private medical insurance is still advised and is essential for all other visitors.

### Dental Services

Dental treatment is expensive in Italy but should be covered by private medical insurance. A list of dentists *(dentisti)* can be found in the yellow pages of the telephone directory.

### Sun Advice

The sunniest (and hottest) months are June, July and August. You are advised to use a strong sunblock and avoid the midday sun.

### Drugs

Prescription and non-prescription drugs and medicines are available from a pharmacy *(farmacia)*, distinguished by a green cross.

### Safe Water

Tap water is generally safe to drink unless marked *acqua non potabile*. Drink plenty of water in hot weather.

## CONCESSIONS

**Students**
Holders of an International Student Identity Card may be able to obtain some concessions on travel, entrance fees, and so on. A 'Venice Card Junior' for those aged 14–30, available from tourist offices, offers discounts in certain hotels, theatres, shops and restaurants as well as a booklet with useful budget information for the young. The main youth hostel in Venice is Ostello Venezia, Fondamenta della Zitelle, on Giudecca (tel: 041 5238211). Reserve well in advance for the summer.

**Senior Citizens**
Venice is a popular destination for older travellers although, due to the limited transport system, you must be prepared for lots of walking. The best deals are available through tour operators who specialize in holidays for senior citizens.

## CLOTHING SIZES

| USA | UK | Europe | |
|---|---|---|---|
| 36 | 36 | 46 | Suits |
| 38 | 38 | 48 | |
| 40 | 40 | 50 | |
| 42 | 42 | 52 | |
| 44 | 44 | 54 | |
| 46 | 46 | 56 | |
| 8 | 7 | 41 | Shoes |
| 8.5 | 7.5 | 42 | |
| 9.5 | 8.5 | 43 | |
| 10.5 | 9.5 | 44 | |
| 11.5 | 10.5 | 45 | |
| 12 | 11 | 46 | |
| 14.5 | 14.5 | 37 | Shirts |
| 15 | 15 | 38 | |
| 15.5 | 15.5 | 39/40 | |
| 16 | 16 | 41 | |
| 16.5 | 16.5 | 42 | |
| 17 | 17 | 43 | |
| 6 | 8 | 34 | Dresses |
| 8 | 10 | 36 | |
| 10 | 12 | 38 | |
| 12 | 14 | 40 | |
| 14 | 16 | 42 | |
| 16 | 18 | 44 | |
| 6 | 4.5 | 38 | Shoes |
| 6.5 | 5 | 38 | |
| 7 | 5.5 | 39 | |
| 7.5 | 6 | 39 | |
| 8 | 6.5 | 40 | |
| 8.5 | 7 | 41 | |

# WHEN DEPARTING

- Contact the airport on the day before leaving to ensure the flight details are unchanged.
- The airport departure tax, payable when you leave Italy, is already included in the cost of the airline ticket.

## LANGUAGE

**Many Venetians speak some English, but they really appreciate it when foreigners make an effort to speak Italian, however badly. It is relatively straightforward to have a go at some basics, as the words are pronounced as they are spelt. Every vowel and consonant (except 'h') is sounded and, as a general rule, the stress falls on the penultimate syllable. Here is a basic vocabulary to help with the most essential words and expressions.**

| | | | |
|---|---|---|---|
| hotel | *albergo* | breakfast | *prima colazione* |
| room | *camera* | toilet | *toilette* |
| ..single/double | *....singola/doppia* | bath | *bagno* |
| ..one/two nights | *per una/due notte/i* | shower | *doccia* |
| | | balcony | *balcone* |
| ..one/two people | *....per una/due persona/e* | reception | *reception* |
| | | key | *chiave* |
| reservation | *prenotazione* | room service | *servizio da camera* |
| rate | *tariffa* | chambermaid | *cameriera* |

| | | | |
|---|---|---|---|
| bank | *banco* | bank note | *banconota* |
| exchange office | *cambio* | coin | *moneta* |
| post office | *posta* | credit card | *carta di credito* |
| cashier | *cassiere/a* | traveller's cheque | *assegno turistico* |
| foreign exchange | *cambio con l'estero* | cheque book | *libretto degli assegni* |
| foreign currency | *valuta estera* | | |
| pound sterling | *sterlina* | exchange rate | *tasso di cambio* |
| American dollar | *dollaro* | commission charge | *commissione* |

| | | | |
|---|---|---|---|
| restaurant | *ristorante* | starter | *il primo* |
| café | *caffè* | main course | *il secondo* |
| table | *tavolo* | dish of the day | *piatto del giorno* |
| menu | *menù/carta* | dessert | *dolci* |
| set menu | *menù turístico* | drink | *bevanda* |
| wine list | *lista dei vini* | waiter | *cameriere* |
| lunch | *pranzo/colazione* | waitress | *cameriera* |
| dinner | *cena* | the bill | *conto* |

| | | | |
|---|---|---|---|
| aeroplane | *aeroplano* | ..single/return | *....andata sola/ andata e ritorno* |
| airport | *aeroporto* | | |
| train | *treno* | ...first/second class | *....prima/seconda classe* |
| ..station | *....stazione ferroviaria* | ticket office | *biglietteria* |
| bus | *autobus* | timetable | *orario* |
| ..station | *....autostazione* | seat | *posto* |
| ferry | *traghetto* | non-smoking | *vietato fumaro* |
| ticket | *biglietto* | reserved | *prenotato* |

| | | | |
|---|---|---|---|
| yes | *sì* | help! | *aiuto!* |
| no | *no* | today | *oggi* |
| please | *per favore* | tomorrow | *domani* |
| thank you | *grazie* | yesterday | *ieri* |
| hello | *ciao* | how much? | *quanto?* |
| goodbye | *arrivederci* | expensive | *caro* |
| goodnight | *buona notte* | open | *aperto* |
| sorry | *mi dispiace* | closed | *chiuso* |

# INDEX

**Acknowledgements**
The Automobile Association would like to thank the following libraries, photographers and agencies for their assistance in the preparation of this title.

**CAFFE FLORIAN 34c, 72c; MARY EVANS PICTURE LIBRARY 14b; LA FENICE © MICHELE CROSERA 68b; WORLD PICTURES 89b**

The remaining photographs are held in the Assocation's own library (AA WORLD TRAVEL LIBRARY) and were taken by ANNA MOCKFORD & NICK BONETTI with the exception of 88c which was taken by PETE BENNETT; 5, 6t, 7t, 7b, 8t, 9t, 10t, 14t, 16/17, 17c, 22b, 23c, 25b, 37c, 39b, 43c, 55, 67c, 67b, 71, 78b, 117t which were taken by SIMON McBRIDE; 12c, 40c, 42b, 44c, 59c, 65b, 74, 80c, 86c, 91-116 which were taken by DARIO MITERDIRI and 8b, 9b, 20c, 22c, 37b, 63b, 66b, 68bl, 69c, 75, 76b, 77, 78t, 79t, 79bl, 79br, 80t, 80b, 81t, 82, 83, 84, 85, 86t, 87t, 87b, 88t, 89t and 117b which were taken by CLIVE SAWYER

**Editorial management:** Apostrophe S Limited

# *Dear Essential Traveller*

**Your comments, opinions and recommendations are very important to us. So please help us to improve our travel guides by taking a few minutes to complete this simple questionnaire.**

*You do not need a stamp (unless posted outside the UK). If you do not want to cut this page from your guide, then photocopy it or write your answers on a plain sheet of paper.*

*Send to*: **The Editor, AA World Travel Guides, FREEPOST SCE 4598, Basingstoke RG21 4GY.**

## Your recommendations...

We always encourage readers' recommendations for restaurants, nightlife or shopping—if your recommendation is used in the next edition of the guide, we will send you a ***FREE* AA *Essential* Guide** of your choice. Please state below the establishment name, location and your reasons for recommending it.

________________________________________

________________________________________

________________________________________

________________________________________

Please send me **AA *Essential*** ________________________

## About this guide...

Which title did you buy?
AA *Essential* ________________________
Where did you buy it? ________________________
When? m m / y y

Why did you choose an AA *Essential* Guide? ________________________

________________________________________

________________________________________

________________________________________

________________________________________

Did this guide meet your expectations?
Exceeded ☐ Met all ☐ Met most ☐ Fell below ☐
Please give your reasons ________________________

________________________________________

________________________________________

________________________________________

*continued on next page...*

Were there any aspects of this guide that you particularly liked? ________

______________________________________________

______________________________________________

Is there anything we could have done better? ________

______________________________________________

______________________________________________

## About you...

Name (*Mr/Mrs/Ms*) ______________________

Address ______________________

______________________________________________

______________________ Postcode ______________

Daytime tel nos ______________________

Please only give us your mobile phone number if you wish to hear from us about other products and services from the AA and partners by text or mms.

Which age group are you in?

Under 25 ☐ 25–34 ☐ 35–44 ☐ 45–54 ☐ 55–64 ☐ 65+ ☐

How many trips do you make a year?

Less than one ☐ One ☐ Two ☐ Three or more ☐

Are you an AA member? Yes ☐ No ☐

## About your trip...

When did you book? m m / y y When did you travel? m m / y y

How long did you stay? ______________________

Was it for business or leisure? ______________________

Did you buy any other travel guides for your trip?

If yes, which ones? ______________________

Thank you for taking the time to complete this questionnaire. Please send it to us as soon as possible, and remember, you do not need a stamp (*unless posted outside the UK*).

*Happy Holidays!*

The information we hold about you will be used to provide the products and services requested and for identification, account administration, analysis, and fraud/loss prevention purposes. More details about how that information is used is in our privacy statement, which you'll find under the heading "Personal Information" in our terms and conditions and on our website: www.theAA.com. Copies are also available from us by post, by contacting the Data Protection Manager at AA, Fanum House, Basing View, Basingstoke, Hampshire RG21 4EA.

We may want to contact you about other products and services provided by us, or our partners (by mail, telephone) but please tick the box if you DO NOT wish to hear about such products and services from us by mail or telephone. ☐